MISSING ™ SPIRITED AWAY

Book 1

Story by
Gakuto Coda

POP
FICTION

A  Prose Novel

TOKYOPOP Inc.
5900 Wilshire Boulevard, Suite 2000
Los Angeles, CA 90036
www.TOKYOPOP.com

Story	Gakuto Coda
Translation	Andrew Cunningham
Cover & Interior Design	Jose Macasocol, Jr.
Layout	Courtney H. Geter
Creative Director	Anne Marie Horne
Senior Editor	Jenna Winterberg

Editor	Kara Allison Stambach
Pre-Press Supervisor	Erika Terriquez
Digital Managing Editor	Chris Buford
Production Manager	Liz Brizzi
Managing Editor	Vy Nguyen
Editor-in-Chief	Rob Tokar
Publisher	Mike Kiley
President and COO	John Parker
CEO & Chief Creative Officer	Stuart Levy

ISBN: 978-1-4278-0032-9

First TOKYOPOP printing: November 2007
10 9 8 7 6 5 4 3 2 1
Printed in the USA

Library of Congress Cataloging-in-Publication Data
Koda, Gakuto, 1977-
  [Missing. English]
  Missing / by Gakuto Coda ; [translated by Andrew Cunningham].
     v <1> cm.
  ISBN-13: 978-1-4278-0032-9 (v. 1 : alk. paper) [1. Missing persons--Fiction. 2. Fantasy.]
I. Cunningham, Andrew, 1979- II. Title.
PZ7.K81747Mi 2007
[Fic]--dc22
                                                                           2007020601

Table of Contents

Prologue:

Beneath the Cherry Grove in Full Bloom

Was their meeting coincidence or fate? Is there really much difference between the two?

First, there was a faint scent . . . drifting on the breeze, carried through the school grounds, past the swaying branches.

When he caught that scent, it brought such a strong sense of déjà vu that Kyoichi Utsume, who had been lying on a bench, sat up abruptly.

The scent was from long ago. It seemed wildly out of place amid the cherry blossoms dancing on the spring breeze. If it wasn't his imagination, then this smell—like withered grass with just a trace of rusted iron—was a smell from his memory. The smell didn't belong at this school.

It was an aromatic memory. . . .

The sense of smell is far more important than people realize in their perceptions of the world. For example, the smell of the moist earth and vegetation after it rains might bring back memories of the garden at your grandfather's house, where you played as a child. Anyone who has experienced something like this will know the feeling.

It needn't be anything that distinct. Going about daily life, people frequently catch a familiar smell, causing them to tilt their heads and wonder what it could be. That was it exactly; the sense of déjà vu this scent gave Utsume was precisely that sensation.

If there was a difference, it was that the memory at the root of this sensation was far gloomier than most childhood memories. That was the only difference, though.

The scent beckoned to him, tugging at his memories.

He turned his nose to the wind. The source of the scent was upwind, and the aroma of the cherry blossoms fluttering through the air all over campus mixed with the dry scent, almost overwhelming it.

Utsume stood up, turning his slim, black-clad frame into the wind to follow the smell. He passed through a grove of trees. Then, a clearing spread out before him. And there . . .

There stood a girl.

"Now the petals scatter,
Let us play between the breeze.
See a girl's dream in the flowers,
Slip between the wind.
A creature dances, dressed in the wind,
Which carries the scent of people.
It sings, wearing shackles that no human can touch.
Playing in the scent of flowers,
Longing for the scent of humans,
The wind maiden sings,
Of sadness beyond human understanding."

She sang, her voice clear, translucent. The wind wrapped her in flower petals.

The girl stood in the center of the clearing by the club building, singing, looking like an impossibly beautiful painting.

Her song felt very old. It was a song, it was a poem, it was a spell. A song of the soul, it expressed everything she felt.

The song lacked a certain polish. The girl was improvising the words and rhythm.

Her voice had resonance, yet it was strangely fragile, melting into the air. As if called by the loneliness in her song, a mysterious wind danced around her, carrying flowers and her scent, playing with her long hair, her clothes, her skirt. It made a stage for her. Everything existed for her benefit—as if no one except her was allowed to be there.

She was completely alone.

Utsume's eyes narrowed in suspicion. He'd noticed something very strange. The space between the club building and the new school building usually was filled with a large number of students coming and going. A bulletin board in front of the new building and several benches placed around it were enough to make it a popular spot to hang out. It also was close to the locker rooms for the sports teams, and large enough that somebody or other always was playing something there; at the moment, several students were playing basketball. At a glance, there were at least ten people there: Some were reading, some were talking, some were sitting, and some were walking past on their way somewhere else. The clearing was hardly empty. Yet . . .

No one looked at the girl, not even the people playing basketball around her—despite that she was standing there and singing, her behavior much too strange to ignore. The only possible explanation was that nobody could see her. She attracted no more attention than the air.

She herself wasn't paying any attention to the people around her. Even when one of the basketball players brushed right past her while chasing after a stray ball, she ignored him, as if neither one could see the other. If they had touched, they almost certainly would have been injured, yet neither seemed aware of the danger.

It was as if everyone else—no, it was as if she herself was an illusion, like she didn't actually exist.

The people around her never looked at her, never touched her, simply passed by as if she weren't there, as if their bodies were passing through one another, as if she were cut out of her surroundings.

A gust of wind blew past . . . and Utsume's expression changed. The wind brought the girl's scent. Utsume caught it, faintly but surely. The scent was of unnatural autumn. He was sure of it. Withered grass and dry rust—the smell that brought him here.

In that instant, Utsume understood: where the girl had come from, who she was, what her true nature was. In that instant, he realized that he understood everything about her. He understood it and accepted it. Not only that, he walked directly over to her and stood in front of her.

The girl was very surprised.

This might seem like an ordinary reaction, but her surprise was not that of a girl suddenly approached by a strange boy.

She looked up at Utsume. Her expression was no longer surprised. "You can . . . see me?"

"Yes."

"Oh!"

It was a puzzling exchange. Nobody listening would've been able to understand the meaning. And there were many people around them. Not one of them thought their conversation was strange. No one even looked at them.

Utsume and the girl stared at each other.

At length, the girl looked sad. "Don't," she whispered.

"Why not?"

"Don't come near me. If you're with me, you'll become like me. You won't be able to return," she offered feebly, along with a sad smile—an awfully tired, faint smile for a girl who looked only about fourteen or fifteen.

Utsume remained expressionless.

"Please," she said. "Forget you ever saw anything. I—"

"I know," Utsume said, interrupting her.

"Eh?"

"I know what you are," Utsume announced.

She looked confused.

He stared directly into her eyes.

"And knowing, I ask: Will you come with me?"

She gazed up at him, stunned.

"I accept your isolation, your nature, all influence you may have on me. I know very well what it means to walk with you." Utsume held out his hand to her. "Come with me."

"No," she said, stepping backward. "No, you don't know. You don't know what I am. You don't know what will happen to you." She shook her head. "I'm nothing but a monster."

Utsume grasped her shoulders. She shuddered.

"Even so, I want you."

Her body went limp.

The mood around them changed. The ball bounced across the ground, with no one to catch it. The boys playing basketball abandoned their game, as if they'd just now noticed Utsume and the girl standing there. They looked shocked, as if the couple suddenly had appeared in the center of the field. Because that was exactly what had happened.

Most of the people nearby never noticed, but a few had seen it happen. They, too, were staring, astounded.

Utsume felt the shift in the world around them, felt them shift back into synch. You know the expression "in their own world"? That's how Utsume had perceived the experience.

In that instant, the world returned to normal, as if waking from a dream. But it had been real. Utsume held the proof of that in his hands: The girl was pressed against his chest.

Supporting her listless frame, Utsume caught the scent of withered grass from her hair. The scent fascinated him, like a drug.

"I was waiting for you," he said.

The girl lowered her eyes. "I'm sorry," she said, almost crying. "I'm sorry." It was not rejection. It was an apology.

Utsume said nothing.

The wind swept around them. It roughly whipped around the girl's hair, spreading out the unseasonable scent of autumn around her.

That was all there was to it. No matter how mysterious it was, no matter how significant an event it was, what happened was nothing more than that.

Chapter 1:

Thus Spoke the Dark Prince

One

"The number you have dialed is currently unavailable."

Takemi Kondou hung up his cell phone in irritation.

He'd just heard his friend Utsume had a new girlfriend. Naturally, he'd called to make fun of him—but even though Utsume should've been somewhere on campus, the call failed to go through.

Takemi made a show of shaking his head at Utsume's luck before sitting down again.

The Literature Club room was on the second floor of the club building. Fourth period had finished some time ago, and not much time was left in the mid-day break.

Seisou Academy, Seisou University's high school, was located in a small city on the Boso Peninsula in Hazama. The brick buildings gave the school a dignified appearance. It wasn't as old and "established" as it looked; however, Seisou was one of the first high schools in Japan to go on the credit system, and the school had a reputation for encouraging independence.

The uniform was a blazer. With the exception of a few ceremonial occasions, it was not required. Some eighty percent of students attended in their own clothes, and the classes tended to have more of a college look than a high school one. Propelled along by the city's efforts to sell itself as an academic town, the scale of the facilities was far beyond that of the average high school.

Students came from all across the country to stay in the enormous dormitories, and the school sported a full range of cultural and athletic resources. The campus was spacious, with all kinds of buildings—including the club building, which was two stories tall, with about twenty rooms. The rooms largely were occupied by cultural clubs that didn't need any specialized facilities. The Literature Club's room was among these.

Takemi and the other second-year students were regulars here.

By the second year, most students had figured out a few tricks, such as avoiding fifth-period classes. Because the cafeteria was still open, they could enjoy a quiet lunch while everyone else was in class.

For Takemi and the others, the mid-day break was spent waiting for the cafeteria to empty.

This trick worked only in the second year: First year students hadn't figured it out yet, and they had inflexible schedules because of too many required credits, anyway. And third-year students, who were concentrating on their exams, couldn't afford the time. Well versed in the school and not yet tackling exam hell, the second-year students were the most relaxed and had the most freedom of anyone in the school.

The mid-day break became a time for them to hang out with friends. And it was during this time that the news of Utsume's girlfriend broke.

◎ ◎ ◎

"Listen, Kondou. Romantic feelings are nothing more than a delusion, merely an extension of possessiveness. Because the object of these feelings is a human, these feelings have been beautified excessively—but underneath, it's simply material desire. The only real merit to romantic behavior hinges on the fact that it's impossible to truly possess another human. It's a rather philosophical value. Why this is so interesting is beyond my understanding."

Once before, Utsume had delivered this speech to Takemi. This was the most famous of Utsume's theories. Utsume had many such theories, but this particular one had stirred up the most controversy. He'd once conducted a fierce argument with an older student who identified himself as a "romantic fundamentalist." They'd eventually agreed to disagree, but first Utsume had rejected the other student's arguments with a single word before proceeding to tear apart what the older student described as a "wonderful emotion," without letting him get a word in edgewise.

Everyone who knew Utsume also came to know him as the man who denied the existence of love. All of them were certain he never would fall for anyone. So, when they heard that Utsume had a girlfriend, even Toshiya was surprised. Aki was amazed, and Takemi sat around muttering things like, "At last, the Prince of Darkness rejoins society!"—all of which might otherwise be considered a mild overreaction.

"Is she cute?" Takemi asked.

"Yeah, really, really cute," stated Ryoko, the source of the information, sounding understandably excited.

"Love, morals, religion—everything generally believed to be of spiritual value is actually a fraud. The moment we place special value on desires and behavior that occur naturally in all humans, vulgar values begin attaching themselves one after the other, transforming the value into a powerful, dangerous poison.

"Environmental protectionism is a hideous concept. To the Earth, mankind is a temporary occupant that soon will cease to exist. Preserving the environment to protect human existence is natural, but is there anything more appalling than when that

nature transforms into misplaced benevolence—for nature, for animals—and into self-righteousness?"

Like Takemi, Kyoichi Utsume was one of the Literature Club's best writers. His writing proved his complete lack of faith in love, affection, or human innocence.

Utsume was extremely strange. He never wore anything but black. He rejected society. You could call him handsome, but the coldness in his gaze destroyed the effect. He was very intelligent; however, his knowledge base leaned heavily toward matters of the occult, witch trails, abnormal psychology—dark subjects.

Because of this, shortly after he met Takemi and the other members of the Literature Club, he was given the nickname "Dark Prince." Takemi was of the opinion that it was impossible to come up with a better nickname for Utsume. When Utsume stood up to explain his radical theories in extremely decisive tones, he looked for all the world like a demonic overlord standing before his armies of darkness and declaring humanity's downfall.

Nobody remembered clearly who had given him the name; it may well have been Takemi. Takemi liked strange people. You could say that he had an unconditional respect for strange people. Takemi considered himself to be distinctly normal, and so he had great admiration for those who were naturally gifted, which had grown into a love of eccentrics. Takemi firmly believed that true genius made people extremely weird.

It was fun watching eccentrics, especially those with the talent to back it up. Eccentrics easily could do things normal people would never think to do—or wouldn't do even if the idea occurred to them. Takemi envied that, and he took pleasure in watching it happen.

Eccentrics' words and actions spit in the face of common sense. Hearing and seeing this was Takemi's greatest joy. For him, being around people like that was more fun than anything else in life. In that sense, to Takemi, Utsume was on a par with a really large theme park—only Utsume generated far more anecdotes.

At any rate, this was the Literature Club's Prince of Darkness, Kyoichi Utsume. Everyone thought he was crazy, while at the same time acknowledging his intelligence and charisma.

"It boggles the mind," cool, acid-tongued Aki Kidono said, snapping shut the paperback she was reading. "Kyo is basically a psychopath. It'd take nerves of steel to go out with him."

"Hey now," Takemi said. "Don't be mean."

"Oh?" Aki said, taking off her glasses and putting them in her case. "Am I wrong?"

"Well, no . . ."

Aki described herself as a "bookworm brought up wrong." She always got right to the point.

Although it might have been merely Takemi's bias, between Aki's flawless fashion sense and her refined appearance and movements, she didn't seem like a bookworm at all. If she held her tongue and grinned, she'd look more like the most popular girl in class.

Every time her mouth opened, though, the words that came out were merciless. And because she was incredibly intelligent, most men found her a little unapproachable.

Her favorite word was "idiots."

Takemi was not alone in his opinion that she stood to gain a lot if she kept quiet. In that sense, she really had been brought up wrong.

"A psychopath? He might be, yeah . . ." Toshiya Murakami muttered, grimacing. "He has the childhood trauma, so it wouldn't surprise me."

His hair cropped short, his skin darkly tanned, Toshiya was nearly six feet tall, making him the least Literature Club-like person there, physically speaking. He and Utsume were childhood friends. Taking little interest in his clothes, he chose the easy route, always wearing his uniform to school. In this way, his sensibility was similar to Utsume with his signature black clothing.

The two apparently had been friends since kindergarten. Their homes were neighboring, and they'd coincidentally ended up at the same high school. So, Toshiya had known Utsume for more than ten years. If Toshiya said it, then there clearly had been something in Utsume's past traumatic enough to cause psychosis.

"He does?" Takemi asked.

"Yeah, well . . ." Toshiya muttered, clearly reluctant to say more.

"Oh, come on!" Takemi's fascination with the alarming always kicked in when people tried to hide something. "We wanna know, right, Kidono?"

"Why are you asking me?" Aki said, looking annoyed. "A little, I suppose—not enough to push."

"Really? I'm totally interested. A guy who's on the edge like Utsume, you gotta wonder how he got like that—as his number one fan."

"It isn't something I should be spreading around."

"Aw . . ." Takemi said, looking dejected.

"Honestly," Aki said, exasperated.

"His Majesty is a good person," Ryoko Kusakabe said, breaking her silence and childishly puffing out her cheeks. "He says scary things, but he's normal! Maybe just a little too smart . . ." she said, seriously trying to defend Utsume.

This cheerful, carefree, popular girl was a member of the "Utsume Fan Club," which Takemi had organized. Counting him, there were exactly two members. They were not actively recruiting.

"I just know he's an amazing person," Ryoko said earnestly.

Aki replied feebly, "Yeah, I wasn't seriously implying Kyo's a lunatic."

"I'll never forget how the Dark Prince's magic saved me from that English test. You all saw it, too!"

This was true. Utsume had used "magic" to help Ryoko.

In their first year, Ryoko's English class had been about to take a minor test. It was the first test she'd taken since high school started, and high school English had been shockingly difficult for her. While she waited for the bell to ring, her stress had mounted until she had a panic attack.

No matter what anyone did, they couldn't calm her down.

Her mind went blank, and she started chanting, "What should I do, what should I do?" over and over to herself, on the verge of tears, as everyone stood around helplessly.

Suddenly, Utsume walked in. He called out, "Kusakabe!" and thrust out his finger, the tip of it stopping a few centimeters away from Ryoko's eyes.

Ryoko froze, staring at his finger.

Everyone watched, surprised.

For a moment, nobody understood what had happened. And then . . .

Her transformation was dramatic. No sooner had her gaze locked onto Utsume's finger than she began to relax visibly. In a few moments, she was completely calm.

The whole stunt had taken less than a minute. It was like magic.

While everyone was still stunned, Utsume went back to his own classroom as if nothing out of the ordinary had happened.

From that day on, no one doubted his nickname.

When Takemi begged him for his secrets, Utsume had explained off-handedly, "That was one method of inducing hypnosis. When someone is confused, their thoughts scattered, the first thing to do is surprise them and give them something to focus on. Anyone can do it. It requires no specialized knowledge or techniques," Apparently, the stunt had been suggested to him by his readings on hypnosis. But knowing this and actually doing it were very different things.

"That was amazing, like real magic," Takemi said, still just as impressed a year later.

"See? Takemi's on my side," Ryoko said proudly, slapping him on the back. "That was obviously magic. I still don't know how he did it!"

"Yeah . . ."

"The Prince of Darkness is *amazing*."

"The Dark Prince's finest hour," Takemi said, looking around for agreement. "Um . . . ?"

Neither Toshiya nor Aki were looking at him. Following their gaze, he and Ryoko turned around—and gasped.

"Ah!"

"Erp . . ."

"I believe my finest hour is yet to come, Kondou," Utsume said, gazing down at them, expressionless as ever.

Two

"Oh, Your Majesty, when did you . . . ?"

"A few minutes ago," Utsume's characteristically intonation-free voice said, cutting off Takemi's attempts to laugh his way off the hook.

"O-oh? I didn't notice."

Utsume gazed down coldly—or rather, unfeelingly—at Takemi. Takemi broke into a cold sweat. He was well aware that this was Utsume's default expression, but that didn't stop his heart from beating as if it were about to burst.

"Y-you should have said!" He looked around for help. Everyone avoided his gaze, grinning. "I hate you all!"

As he squirmed, Takemi was genuinely surprised. He honestly hadn't had any idea that Utsume was standing behind him.

Usually, Utsume's charisma was so powerful, his presence so strong that you could feel it in the air when he entered a room. Some people insisted this was his aura; regardless of the reason, everyone agreed there was something powerful about him, something unlike other people.

It surprised Takemi that, today, this presence had vanished completely. His face, voice, and manner were the same as always, but that feeling had disappeared.

It was unlike Utsume to sneak up on people. He always strode into the wind, putting the utmost confidence into each stride.

"Your phone off? I was trying to call." Takemi said, trying to change the subject.

Utsume cocked his head. "No, it's on."

"Then, I guess it was out of range."

"I suppose."

The students might call it a country school, but it was close enough to the Kanto area that they never had problems with cell phones. If a phone failed to connect, it usually meant it was off.

It seemed that wasn't the case here, though. Not that it was really important. It wasn't what Takemi wanted to talk about. He'd been caught off guard a moment before; now, he could turn the tables. Takemi calmed down and grinned. "So, Your Majesty. I hear you have a girlfriend?" He did his best to leer.

"Mm? Yeah," Utsume said, emotionless.

"You crafty devil. What made your heart melt?"

"It didn't. My beliefs and principles in no way interfere with my possessions."

"Possessions?"

Takemi had been sure he could embarrass Utsume, whose extremely matter-of-fact response had been a surprise. It was as though Utsume had found a dog or a cat by the side of the road. No—if he'd done that, he would've been more emotional. It was more like he'd found a rock.

"Possession? Is that all?"

"What do you mean?"

"What do I—oh, come on!"

Not only was he unembarrassed, he wasn't bothering to try to defend himself. He didn't seem to care.

Takemi was at a loss—and a little disgusted. He sighed. "I can't even make fun of you," he said, disappointed.

Toshiya gave him a sympathetic smile. "You shouldn't have gotten your hopes up."

"Yeah, I know." Takemi muttered forlornly. Then, he frowned: He still hadn't seen the girl.

"So, Utsume, where is the girl? She was with you, right?" Takemi asked.

Ryoko had met Utsume in first period that morning, where she was introduced to his girlfriend. So, there was a good chance the girl was still on campus somewhere. Takemi wanted to meet her, if possible, to see her with his own eyes.

Takemi looked at the empty space around Utsume. "She's not here now?"

Utsume frowned. He stared as if doubting Takemi's sanity. "Kondou . . ."

"Yeah?"

Utsume sighed, thrusting out his finger and pointing at Takemi's brow. Then, he turned the finger to the side, pointing down diagonally.

Takemi looked where Utsume pointed. Their eyes met.

"Augh!" There was a petite girl standing right next to Takemi. He yelped, and the girl squealed back, jumping away from him.

"Ah! Excuse me, I'm sorry!" For some reason, she apologized.

Flustered, she looked from Takemi to Utsume before settling on simply standing there, looking anxious.

She appeared to be a very nervous girl—or more likely, unaccustomed to being around people.

"Oh, sorry!" Takemi said, feeling like he'd done something very wrong.

She was very cute! She looked like she was about a year younger than the rest of them. Long black hair, pale skin—she was an old-fashioned beauty, like a doll.

Not to say that she lacked expression or anything of that sort. But her presence was bizarrely thin and, coupled with her even features and small frame, she gave off a doll-like impression.

With that in mind, the dark red cape and long dress she wore were not very modern looking. However, they looked very natural on her, as if she had been born to wear them.

"See, like I said," Ryoko said, beaming with pride.

Everyone stared at Utsume's girlfriend in astonishment. The feeling in the room was that something completely out of place had popped out suddenly. The girl nervously looked around her, as though she had no idea what was going on.

"Kyo," Aki started, chin in hand, elbow on the windowsill, "she's not right for you," she said bluntly. This was more or less what everyone in the room had been thinking.

Next to the expressionless, haughty Utsume, this meek, uncertain girl seemed somehow unbalanced. The pairing was far too unnatural: No one looking at them would take them for a couple. They seemed too different.

Perhaps "unbalanced" was the wrong word—it was more like they weren't even trying to balance.

Takemi's own opinion was a little more positive, although he still was taken aback. She was certainly cute, but he never would've imagined she was Utsume's type.

Utsume had a tendency to value other people based on nothing except their abilities. If he had imagined Utsume falling for anyone, it would've been someone astonishingly intelligent, ultra capable. This girl, however, seemed inexperienced and sheltered. How had they met?

"Where did you meet her?"

No sooner had he asked than Aki snapped, "Idiot."

"What?"

"Do you normally ask that when meeting someone? Start with her name."

"Huh? Oh! Oh, right!" Now that she mentioned it, Takemi realized he didn't know the girl's name. It wasn't that he'd forgotten to ask. It was more like, for some reason, he'd been certain she didn't have a name. He hadn't doubted that strange conviction.

"Right, yeah." Takemi had no idea why he'd thought this. Between that and not having noticed her standing there, he really wasn't at his best today.

"You feeling okay, Takemi?" Ryoko asked.

He grinned reassuringly at her, got a grip, and turned back to the girlfriend.

"Sorry, don't know what I was thinking. What's your name?"

She said nothing. She simply stood there, looking confused.

"She hates you!" Ryoko teased.

"Prince . . ." Takemi said, looking to Utsume for help.

Utsume frowned, concerned. "Ayame. That's her name. She's sixteen."

"Oh? Only a year younger than me!" Takemi said, surprised.

It was the middle of April, and Takemi's birthday was April 1st, which made him the oldest person in the room.

She was that old? Takemi had thought she was two or three years younger. Her intense shyness might have made her seem younger, and she was shorter than average. Takemi knew full well that people aged at different speeds.

"Old name," Aki said, so sharply it sounded a little hostile. "I mean, it's unusual," she said, noticing this herself and trying to correct it.

"Utsume," Takemi said, "That might work for Your Majesty, but the rest of us can't call her by her first name like that." He made sure to keep his tone mocking.

Utsume frowned, not following his drift, like it had never occurred to him that people in Japan who weren't well acquainted didn't call one another by their first names.

Takemi suppressed a chuckle. "I mean," he grinned. "What's her last name?" It seemed like a natural question to him, asking her name.

Utsume looked absolutely dumbfounded for a second. His expression rapidly changed to that of someone who has made a terrible mistake. A moment later, his face stiffened, and he looked down sharply at Ayame. His eyes were always a little cold; now, they were positively sinister.

"Uh . . . ?" Takemi had no idea what was going on.

Utsume appeared to be extremely annoyed. Takemi has seen this happen only a handful of times, all of them when Utsume had screwed up somehow.

It wasn't that Takemi's question displeased him—nothing like that. Utsume didn't get annoyed by other people, because he never expected anything from them in the first place. That meant Utsume had made some sort of horrible blunder. And as always, the source of his irritation was totally beyond the comprehension of his friends.

Utsume's stare unsettled Ayame still further. She shook her head, looking very upset.

Utsume thought for a moment.

There was a strange silence.

Takemi had no idea what this quick exchange of body language implied; but a moment later, Ayame opened her mouth to say something, and Utsume stopped her. He turned around as if nothing at all had happened, saying casually, "Kondou."

"Huh?"

"Her name's Kondou. Same as yours. Ayame Kondou," Utsume said, obviously forced.

Takemi was totally lost now. "Really?" he said, regarding Ayame.

Ayame seemed a little stunned. She looked up at Takemi like a frightened rabbit.

Then, she gave a little shake and said, "Y-yes. Yes. Ayame . . . Kondou." Then, she nodded to herself several times. She seemed extremely flustered. "Uh, um . . . nice to meet you!" she squeaked, bowing so suddenly that she smacked her head on Takemi's chest. "Eek!"

"Whoops!"

"Ah! Augh! I'm very sorry!"

"Mm? Oh no, don't worry about it," Takemi said, growing embarrassed himself.

Now that he heard it again, her voice was remarkably clear and beautiful. The disconnect with her awkward words was oddly cute. She's perfect, Takemi thought: the embodiment of cute, a perfect beauty. He knew people like this existed and had seen them on television, but it was the first time he'd actually met one. He expected nothing less from the Dark Prince's girlfriend. And oddly enough, he wasn't at all jealous.

Both Ayame and Utsume had something otherworldly about them, and it was hard for him to think of them as something he could reach out and touch. It was like the gap the average citizen feels between himself and highly ranked politicians, or like the distance the average mind feels between itself and genius.

He asked again, "Where did you meet?"

He didn't really expect an answer, but Utsume instantly gave him one he never would have seen coming: "I found her."

"Found her?" Takami gaped stupidly. "Where's she from?"

"What do you mean?"

"Her school, where she lives . . ."

"No idea."

"No idea? Then, did you . . ." Takemi stammered.

"Did you kidnap her?" Ryoko said gleefully. "Nice one, Your Majesty!"

"In a sense. Don't worry, I broke no laws."

"The perfect crime?"

"That's not what I meant."

"Hold on a second," Takemi said, interrupting this increasingly strange conversation. If things kept up like this, he never would get the drift. "You know only her name?"

"Yeah."

"When did you meet?"

"Yesterday."

"And she's your girlfriend?"

"She is."

This was insane. Yet Utsume never wavered.

"Don't you want to know more? Don't you need to know more?"

"No. If she wants to tell me, she will, and I won't stop her. I myself don't feel moved to pry."

"Isn't that strange?"

"How so?"

"In every way! Absolutely!"

"Specifically?"

"Specifically . . ." Takemi stammered. He couldn't quite put his finger on it. "What do you think?" he asked, changing the object of his questions. "Utsume doesn't know anything about you, how much do you know about him? Doesn't it bother you not knowing anything about each other?"

Ayame hesitated, finding herself suddenly in the spotlight. She wavered for a moment; then, her lips tensed with resolve, and she said, "I don't care. I already made up my mind."

Takemi was silenced. He didn't know what she meant, but her expression was so earnest, so intent.

"Satisfied?" Utsume asked. "If you're through interrogating her . . ."

He already was turning to leave—or possibly to flee.

"You have somewhere to be?" Aki asked.

Utsume jerked his chin at Ayame. "Yeah. I'm introducing her to everyone I know."

"That's unlike you."

"Possibly so," he said, leaving the room. Ayame followed a few steps behind.

"Wait!" Takemi said, calling after her.

Utsume might not be interested in knowing more about her, but Takemi was, as most normal people would be. It was normal to want to know more about the people you met, know who they were. So, he asked, "Where are you from?"

Ayame turned around. She hesitated for a moment, a little worried, thinking about something. She glanced back at the hallway: Utsume wasn't waiting for her. Sounding deeply apologetic, she said, "I'm sorry. It's a secret." Then, she turned and darted after Utsume.

"Ah," Takemi said. Before he could ask anything else, she was out of sight down the hall.

Three

For a while, everyone stared pointlessly at the door through which Utsume and his girlfriend had left. They all seemed lost in thought, and a strange silence settled on the room.

"Man, the Prince of Darkness is weird," Takemi muttered. The Dark Prince's girlfriend had been even stranger than he had dared hope—by which he meant "interesting."

"Told you she was cute," Ryoko declared, almost bragging.

"Yeah, that's true enough."

"See? What'd you think, Murakami? You didn't say anything."

"Mm? Hm. Yeah . . ." Toshiya said, looking up. He sounded as if he'd been only half-listening.

Ever since Utsume had come by and introduced Ayame, Toshiya had been leaning on the bookshelf with his arms folded, silently glowering.

"Something bothering you, Murakami?" Takemi asked.

"Nothing. Forget about it," Toshiya said, waving his hand. Even as he spoke, he seemed lost in thought.

"Murakami," Aki called. Aki's expression was just as grim. She gave Toshiya a meaningful look.

Toshiya nodded.

"What? What's going on?" Ryoko said, looking from one to the other. Neither said anything.

Ryoko kept staring until Toshiya said, "Oh, just . . ." and trailed off again.

Something was wrong, obviously.

"Seriously, what's wrong, you two?" Takemi said forcefully.

Aki said nothing, simply glaring at the floor as if mulling over something.

Takemi's heart fluttered; he wasn't sure if it was out of curiosity or anxiety.

At last, Aki looked up. "Kondou," she said before hesitating again, as if she couldn't decide if she should say it or not. While she tried to make up her mind, she repeated Kondou's name, followed by, "When you first saw that girl, what did you think?"

"Huh? I dunno. She was cute?"

"No," Aki shook her head. "Not that. At first, you didn't notice she was there, right? You noticed only after Kyo pointed at her. What did you feel then, at that moment?"

"Um, I was surprised? She didn't make a noise, and I didn't notice her there at all. Then, our eyes met. I thought, 'where was I looking?'"

"Hm . . ."

"What?"

Aki looked at Toshiya. He opened his mouth. "It wasn't just you, Kondou. I didn't notice she was there, either. Neither did Kidono, nor Kusakabe, probably. It was more like we were able to see her all of a sudden. It might just be our imagination; if not, though, something very, very wrong just happened."

"Exactly. It was like that girl had been standing in my blind spot. But there are four of us here—me, Kondou, Murakami, Kusakabe. That girl was standing in *everyone's* blind spot, except for Kyo's. None of us noticed she was there. Did you see her, Ryoko?"

Everyone looked at Ryoko, who said, "Of course I did."

"You did? Okay, then," and everyone relaxed. Except . . .

"No, not just now," Toshiya said abruptly. "You met Utsume first period, and he introduced her there. Could you see her the whole time then? Or did you notice her only after he introduced her?"

Ryoko thought hard, frowning.

Takemi stood up. "Wait, what does that—"

"Kondou, shut up," Aki snapped.

Takemi sat down again.

Toshiya watched Ryoko. "Well?"

Ryoko thought a moment longer, dubious. She didn't want to admit it, given the obviously negative reaction to Ayame. "It's just a coincidence. She's so small and quiet. . . ."

"Did you see her?" Aki said, brushing aside Ryoko's excuses. "Did you?"

"No," Ryoko said reluctantly.

"B-but what does . . . ?" Takemi asked. He was totally lost.

"I don't know. However, we should be on guard. There's something very wrong here," Aki said calmly. "I'm not saying we should do anything. If it was a coincidence, then fine. I just hope he hasn't been captured by some sort of ghost, that's all. Watch her carefully. You too, Kondou—make sure your beloved Dark Prince isn't dragged off anywhere."

"Ghost? Kidono!" Takemi exclaimed, looking at Aki. She must've been joking, but she wasn't smiling at all. "But that's imposs—"

"I was joking—or I wish I had been. You saw her. Can you say for sure she wasn't a ghost? That was like horror movie camera work," Aki said, standing up. "I'm going to lunch. Keep this conversation in this room. Don't tell anyone else, and make sure Kyo and that girl don't hear about it."

She left.

"I'll see you there," Toshiya said, following after her.

Left alone, Takemi and Ryoko looked at each other. There was a long silence.

"What do you think?" Takemi asked.

"Mm . . . I don't know."

"It's not jealousy—neither one of them is the type."

"Yeah . . ."

To Takemi, both Aki and Toshiya always seemed far more grown-up than he was. They both knew the extent of their own abilities and were confident in them. Their grades, the things they thought about, the things they wrote for the club 'zine—Takemi couldn't come close to them. Takemi was the jealous one. With talent like theirs, they needn't ever be jealous of other people. *That's* what made him jealous.

"A ghost?"

"Nah, she can't be. Aki didn't really believe that either."

"I hope not. Why else would Kidono and Murakami be so tense, though?"

"Hm . . ." Ryoko said. "Whatever. They don't like the Dark Prince's girlfriend. That's what it basically comes down to. That's His Majesty's business, though, and it's not like he's gonna bring her every day, even though this school isn't very strict about letting in outsiders. It'll be fine."

"I guess so. It's a bit awkward, though."

"Yeah, I know," Ryoko said, closing the window. "Let's go eat lunch. It's not worth thinking about. The whole mess is for the dogs, and I'd hate to miss eating because of it," she said, flashing her teeth.

"Yeah," Takemi said, grinning. They could think about it later.

"Come on."

"Sure," Takemi said, drawing the curtains shut to block out the sunlight, following the club rules.

Chapter 2:

Thus Spoke the Ghost Girl

One

"Let's follow them."

Ryoko Kusakabe didn't say this out of curiosity or a sense of duty. Classes had ended, and they were out of school. While standing at the stop for the bus headed into town, she spotted Utsume and Ayame in the crowd of students by pure coincidence.

"Good idea!" Takemi said, as Ryoko had known he would.

It wasn't strictly accurate to say obligation and curiosity played no part, but the main reason Ryoko had suggested tailing them was because she knew Takemi would love it.

Aki had gone to the library to look up something. If the club wasn't meeting, Toshiya always went right home to help his family's business. And unless someone specifically invited him to do something, Utsume usually wandered off quickly, as well— which he was doing now.

Ryoko was pleased with her idea, and her heart beat quickly in anticipation.

The city of Hazama had a population of about fifty thousand people, barely large enough to qualify as a city. Beyond the beach was Hazama Harbor. Inland from the tiny harbor, the ground rose progressively, so the entire city was built on a gentle slope. The buildings were old but western style. City ordinance protected the sandstone-tile buildings that lined the rows, so you could walk in the inner part of the old city from the harbor to Seisou University and feel as if you'd come unstuck in time.

The origins of the city were rather unusual. It originally had been nothing more than a fishing village. It began functioning as a city during the Meiji era, when it was intended to host a number of villas for visiting foreigners. Thus, all the buildings were designed following western construction, which was very rare at the time. For many reasons, the buildings barely were used for their original purpose; and as a result, Hazama remained a very un-Japanese-looking city.

Cobblestone streets, sandstone-tile walls, magnificent gabled roofs . . . fortunate enough to have avoided destruction by earthquakes and war, the city worked to preserve the look of the town, with strict restrictions on buildings that might damage tourism. Essentially, the entire city became a tourist attraction, especially the center of it.

While the buildings were old, they were not old enough to qualify as cultural treasure. To protect them, there were few roads or train lines, making buses the main means of public transportation.

Hazama was also an academic town.

As its origins would suggest, Hazama had no industry to speak of. Money from tourism hardly could be counted on, because the history and location of the town fatally lacked any strong selling point. Its tourism campaigns calling the city "the new Kobe" or "the new Nagasaki" had ended in failure, and Hazama had long since lost the fishing industry. The main use of the harbor was the docks for ferryboats and flocks of amateur fishermen. Although tourism was the reason they had worked so hard to preserve the look of the town, it failed to generate much revenue.

The only choice the town had left was to promote academics. Taking advantage of the surroundings, they were able to attract good schools, filling the town with students.

That brings us to the present: The city's decisions had paid off. The enormous Seisou University had set itself up here, branched off into a high school and junior high, and become the linchpin of the town's economy. The town was filled with dormitories.

Cobblestone roads and students everywhere you looked— this was the academic city of Hazama.

Among that academic crowd, Ryoko and Takemi followed their targets, spending thirty minutes on a bus packed with students.

Utsume and Ayame got off the bus in front of Hazama station and turned into the shopping arcades off the main road. The arcade was still new and was said to look like similar roads in Italy. This was a windfall from the town's beautification ordinances; the town still was courting the tourist dollar.

It was quiet, but hardly empty.

Utsume and Ayame walked on, moving steadily away from it. They obviously weren't here to shop.

"Huh? Where'd they go?"

"Takemi, over there."

"Mm? Oh! Thanks." Takemi was having trouble keeping them in sight. "Sorry."

"Keep looking around like that and you'll lose them again."

"Eh? Augh! I have!"

"See?" Ryoko said, grinning. In truth, she had no desire to criticize him. She was having trouble keeping them in sight herself. No matter how much she concentrated, they would slip into a crowd or into a shadow, vanishing. They were gone before she knew it, and she would have to hunt them down again.

The only reason she'd managed to keep track of them this far was because, as a fashion-conscious woman, her eyes easily picked out clothing. Both Utsume and Ayame were wearing very unique outfits. Regardless, they kept slipping into her blind spot; when she found them again, they would be somewhere else entirely, as if they were teleporting.

Ayame was easy enough to overlook—yet Utsume barely was registering, as well, as though Ayame were draining his aura.

"Lost them again."

"Not there, Takemi. There."

"Wow, I don't know how you do it. The power of jealousy?"

"No . . ." *Argh.* It wasn't. It really wasn't. You see, Ryoko was in love with Takemi.

For no particular reason, Ryoko didn't believe there was any logic to love. Everyone talked about the reason they'd fallen in love or the reasons they liked someone, but Ryoko thought they'd invented that after the fact. One day, she'd simply realized that she was in love. That was all that mattered to her. Making up reasons retroactively only clouded the emotion. If she came to a point that her feelings needed reinforcement, she could look for reasons then.

Of course, Takemi hadn't noticed how she felt.

Ryoko hadn't told anyone. By the time she noticed her own feelings, the two already were good friends and were spending a lot of time together. This was enough for her. She was afraid that telling him would destroy the relationship they had.

Ryoko had begun to think that love did not necessarily demand dramatic developments. There was pleasure to be had in drama, but it was a poisoned dagger in the heart of quiet happiness. What she needed most right now, Ryoko believed, was solid ground under her feet. If events led to them dating, fine. By then, they would be so close that even poison couldn't tear them apart.

If love needed some dramatic trigger to set it off, then Ryoko would have fallen for Utsume instead of Takemi. Utsume's "magic" had been dramatic; but while she had great respect for him, Ryoko had no romantic feelings for Utsume at all.

Utsume wasn't that kind of person. He was something else, something more unique. There was something about Utsume that distanced him from those around him. For example, Utsume had a sort of sixth sense. Everyone around him knew about it.

Once, Ryoko had just come into class, when Utsume looked up from his book and without so much as a 'hello,' said, out of the blue, "You smell like incense, Kusakabe. Were you at a memorial service?"

There had been no memorial service—but there had been something else, which gave Ryoko goose bumps. On her way to school that day, she had seen a bouquet of flowers placed on the side of the road. There must have been an accident. There was an open can of soda, some toys, and some candy placed around the flowers, suggesting that a young child had been run over. How sad, Ryoko thought, and she walked on by.

The incense placed near the flowers had long since turned to ash and looked so forlorn. It had stuck in her mind. . . . That must be it. Of course, if the incense had burned out, the scent couldn't have transferred to Ryoko.

"Dark Prince, can you see something?" she had asked, turning pale.

"No," Utsume said, losing interest and returning his gaze to his book. "The lingering shadow of its mind trailed along after you. Nothing to worry about."

"Dark Prince, you're making me worry . . ."

"Don't. It probably was drawn to your sympathy. It's fading away. It'll be gone soon."

He refused to say anything more, and nothing else out of the ordinary seemed to happen.

If anyone else had said it, she would have laughed it off. She might have accused the person of lying. With Utsume, though, it was natural. He seemed like the type.

There was something fantastic about Utsume. This might be why. However, when she told other people what she felt, they all laughed. Ryoko was greatly annoyed.

"Sorry, Ryoko, lost them again," Takemi said, and Ryoko looked up, surprised.

She had been lost in thought. "Eh? Ah! Oh no!" She hurriedly looked around her, trying to find the couple again.

Two

They had entered a deserted area of town: Utsume turned around one corner after another, without encountering any passersby.

They were now beyond the scope of the town's preservation efforts. The road, just wide enough for a single car to pass, was lined with ordinary homes and apartment buildings, surrounded by gray walls.

Tailing someone was harder than they'd thought. They had no idea how far behind they had to stay to avoid detection. If they stayed a safe distance away, they would lose sight of their targets; if they got too close, they would be seen.

Ryoko's heart beat like a *taiko* drum from the thrill and tension. She was half-convinced it was loud enough for Takemi to hear.

Evening was almost over. The sun had set, and it was growing dark around them. Although the streetlights were coming on, the rows of houses all looked the same, and the light didn't make them any more distinct.

Ryoko was getting nervous. If Takemi hadn't been with her, she would have given up long ago. "Where are we? How will we get home?"

"Dunno. I guess we're going to . . . to Kondou's house," Takemi said. Her name was the same as his, which made him uncomfortable. "I feel like we're being lured somewhere."

Ryoko agreed.

The street had looked the same for a creepily long time. Travelers that were tricked by a *kitsune* and were led round and round over the same ground must feel like this. She'd heard of *onibi* or will-o-the-wisps that did the same kind of thing. If you followed after them, they would lead you around for ages, finally dragging you into a bottomless marsh. Utsume had told her about them.

Ryoko shuddered, banishing the thought from her mind. She was managing only to scare herself.

Being careful not to stand under the street lights, Ryoko concentrated on keeping Utsume in sight.

"Mm? Again?" Takemi shook his head.

Ryoko had lost them, as well.

There were no crowds or anything else that could hide them. Yet they had somehow vanished into the shadows beyond the reach of the streetlights. Utsume was dressed in black, which made it easy to lose him.

It was very dark now.

Ryoko shivered.

It was starting to look like they would find themselves alone, with no idea how to get home. She never thought to knock on a door and ask for directions. An obsessive anxiety, which had been lurking inside for a while now, suddenly was rushing through her entire body, fanning her fear.

She looked around her, flustered. There wasn't a soul in sight, nothing but the feeble light of the streetlights in rows in either direction. They were the only thing that stood out from the darkness. They seemed to stretch away forever.

The walls blocked light coming from the houses, and none of it reached them. It was like they were in some other world, tossing their artificial light toward the sky.

Isolation. Anxiety. Ryoko gabbed a fistful of Takemi's jacket. Even that seemed thin, unfamiliar. And then . . .

"O-over there!" Ryoko cried, pointing. She thought she'd seen something move.

A few blocks ahead of them, she'd seen Ayame turn a corner in the darkness, but not Utsume. Was it too dark? Had he already turned the corner?

It was so dark, they could no longer make out colors. Through the enveloping darkness, Ryoko barely could see the girl; the way she slid around the corner made her look exactly like a ghost.

They gave chase, convinced, somehow, that they had no other choice. Ryoko and Takemi rounded the corner running. Down a narrower road yet, Ayame was turning another corner. They chased her, turning onto a still narrower road. Ayame already was turning the next corner. They ran after her, chasing her through darker and darker roads.

A sudden light blinded them.

It seemed they had come out on the original road—or some other big road. Old streetlights shone a flickering light on the two. Lights stretched out on either side through the darkness.

Flickering.

The lights went way off into the distance, out of sight.

Flickering. Flickering.

Forever, an endless hallway of lights and darkness.

Darkness. Quiet.

The only sound was the hum of the streetlights.

Hush. Silence.

And then, Ryoko saw a human shape: a black figure standing under a distant light. Ryoko let out a little yelp. "Dark Prince . . ."

It was Utsume's slim frame. He had his back to them and was walking away—far, far away, away from the light, into the darkness, and becoming so faint that he seemed on the verge of vanishing as the distance between them increased. He looked like he was melting into the darkness.

She panicked. "Dark Prince!" she tried to shout, but only a whisper came out. Her throat was unnaturally dry, and her voice stuck in it. Beside her, Takemi was swallowing air and gasping.

And then, the darkness swallowed Utsume.

"Dark Prince!"

Horrified at the sight, Ryoko tried to run after him. She took one step forward—and stopped, her heart leaping into her throat. There was a girl standing in front of her.

The darkness laughed: "*Tee hee hee.*"

It was Ayame. Ayame was standing right in front of her.

Ryoko was standing in the light under a streetlight. Just beyond was darkness. Ayame was standing in the darkness, head down. The light from above shone on her, hiding half her face in deep shadows. But her mouth was twisted up into a shape like a smile—an empty, hollow smile.

"*Tee hee hee.*"

Her lips were parted slightly, and from the empty, hollow darkness inside slipped out a laugh, a very unnatural laugh, a motionless laugh—a doll's laugh.

"*Tee hee hee.*"

"Who are—" Ryoko tried to ask. The girl in front of her couldn't possibly be the one she knew.

There was no answer. The air felt tense. Something was wrong. They air they'd been breathing normally now felt strange, oppressive, like it was not from this Earth.

The air itself was steeped in cold fear, built into the unnatural night. All her hairs stood up, letting her sense the night air more, letting the fear reach her better.

She could no longer sweat. Her back was so stiff it hurt. Her body couldn't move. Her chin was trembling.

Ryoko was no longer in the world she knew. This was some other world. If she stepped out of the light, the darkness would wrap about Takemi and her, mercilessly destroying their souls.

The night of fear had begun before they knew it.

Ayame stood with darkness behind her. The light seemed to pull her out of the darkness. Before her, the two of them could not move.

"What . . . are you?" Takemi asked in a strangled voice.

"*Too . . . late . . .*" the darkness said. "*Nothing . . . can save . . .*" It was a fragile voice. And a beautiful one. The beauty was overwhelmed by the fear, turning cold. "*Can never . . . go home . . .*" It was Ayame's voice, echoing through the darkness, melting into the darkness, and they could not tell if it was coming from the girl in front of them. The voice came from nowhere in particular, seeping out of the darkness.

"Can't go home?" Ryoko said, suddenly realizing. "Does that mean—" At first, she'd thought it meant her and Takemi. "Does that mean—" her voice trembled. She had forgotten why they were here. "The one who can't go home . . . is the Dark Prince?"

The darkness laughed quietly, darkly.

> *"Let's go,*
> *Let's go,*
> *Let's go to the other side,*
> *To the hollow kingdom,*
> *The hidden village,*
> *For eternity,*
> *In the darkness,*
> *The sun never sets, crossing the red sky with the moon,*
> *Never-ending twilight, hiding people's faces,*
> *Let's go,*
> *Let's go,*
> *Let's go to the other side."*

"Stop!" Takemi shrieked, seemingly unable to bear the whispered voices, the spell they were chanting.

The darkness snickered.

They could feel them, feel the things shifting in the darkness all around: creeping, crawling, coming closer to them. From the left, from the right, surrounding them. The things stayed out of reach of the light, lurking at the edge of the darkness. Buried in the gloom, they looked like shadow puppets. Ryoko and Takemi were surrounded by a crowd of things they could not quite make out.

The things felt like people, but they couldn't be people: They squirmed, tumbled, struggled, the shapes changing in a sickening fashion. One shrank to the height of a child before stretching taller than the walls. Shifting, shifting, like a sinister shadow theater.

They were made of flesh, masses of misshapen flesh.

"Eek!" Ryoko choked back a scream. Something had grabbed her wrist with frightening strength. She glanced down at her arm, instantly regretting it.

The hand was white, white like the dead, reaching out of the darkness. The owner of the hand was in the darkness. She could see only a shadow. It was small, like a child. Its pulse beat against her skin. Now, she did scream.

Takemi tore the fearsome hand off her, and it was sucked back into the darkness, like a snake fleeing the light.

> *"Come home,*
> *Come home,*
> *To the inhuman homeland,*
> *Things that can't be human, to the inhuman homeland,*
> *Things that lack a human heart, to the inhuman homeland,*
> *Things that lost their humanity, to the inhuman homeland,*
> *All heartless things, to the inhuman homeland—"*

"Stop! Stop!" Takemi screamed, fear and anger mingling in his voice.

He was shaking. Ryoko could feel it through the jacket she clutched. Or was it Ryoko that was shaking?

Fear had all five senses on full alert. Information flooded her body, and she could make no sense of it. It was so very cold.

"We won't give him back.
He is ours now.
His heart is on the other side.
His heart is no longer with you.
We won't give it back.
You can't get it back.
You have neither light nor darkness in hand.
You don't have lanterns, you don't have cat's eyes . . ."

Chatter, chatter. The sound of her teeth chattering echoed inside her head.

"Shut up! You don't even make sense!" Takemi shouted, shuddering.

Fear, anger, terror, confusion.

The darkness continued to shift.

"It's too late. I . . ." Ayame raised her head, and . . . vanished like a candle flame.

Darkness. They remembered nothing else.

Three

"So, we ran and ran—but no matter how far we went, everything looked the same. Same houses, same walls, same lights, forever. 'Scary' isn't the word for it. Man, it just isn't as scary when you try to put it into words."

Takemi desperately was trying to explain their experience to Aki and Toshiya.

Mid-day break, the Literature Club room: Ryoko and the others had gathered like always, except there was nothing usual about what started there today.

Takemi's horror story . . . He was not terribly informative. He spoke passionately but incoherently. The two listening faces were oddly serious, though—for one simple reason: No one had seen Utsume since.

Utsume stood in the darkness,

Utsume melted into the darkness,

His silhouette gradually warped,

His arms bending like clay in horrible directions,

His shoulders twisting to different heights,

Half his face melting away,

His legs, stomach, back turned to something like mud or tentacles, with a horrible slurping noise,

His head turned upside down,

His trunk stretched out, twisting,

"This is what happens to humans who walk with me," Ayame laughed, as his body continued to warp obscenely. . . .

Ryoko woke up. It was morning.

She remembered nothing after that; the next thing she knew, it was morning.

Ryoko woke in her own room. She was wearing pajamas, and the alarm clock went off like always. All her things were ready for the day's classes. So, at first, she believed the events of the night before had been a dream.

Ryoko lived in the dorm. About half the students in the school did, so this was hardly unusual. It was actually more unusual to live at home. Utsume and Toshiya were the only members of the Literature Club that did. Aki was even more unusual: She had an apartment in the city and lived alone. There were rumors that her parents were rich.

So, when Ryoko opened her eyes, she was in her dorm room, left wondering if it all had been a dream. It didn't take her bleary, sleep-fogged mind long to decide it had been.

"Morning," her roommate, Nozomi Nukata said.

"Mornin'," she groaned back.

What an awful dream. That was all the thought Ryoko put into it. She'd been under the covers, but the dream had left her body feeling cold.

"Nozomi, I had a really scary dream . . ." Ryoko said.

Nozomi was well engaged in her morning battle with her unruly hair.

"It was dark . . . and cold . . . and scary . . ."

"It's too early for you to start babbling," Nozomi said, grinning. "Get up, wash that face, and get dressed."

"Okay," she said, slowly hauling herself out of bed. Her body hurt all over. "Ugh, I feel awful . . . because of the dream?"

"You okay?" Nozomi asked, as Ryoko sluggishly pulled on some clothes.

"Yeah, fine."

"Okay, then," Nozomi said, and she went back to brushing.

"That all?"

"Yep." Then, she frowned, remembering something. "Oh yeah, Ryoko, where'd you go last night?"

"Mm? What do you mean?"

"I was worried when you weren't back by curfew. I gave up and went to eat dinner; when I got back, you already were asleep. I could have strangled you."

"Eh? Really?"

"Oh, come on! Don't give me the amnesia routine!"

"Oh, no. Right. Sorry."

"What were you doing?"

"Uh, um . . . sorry, I was just running late."

"Huh." Nozomi snorted, not buying it. "Okay, then. Try not to make me worry again, okay?"

"I'm sorry."

"If anything happens to you, I'll get blamed."

"Right." And she didn't think about it anymore.

She tried to remember more but couldn't, and she was sleepy. She had to hurry to get ready for school.

Ryoko had low blood pressure and hated mornings. She wasn't able to think yet. But she couldn't deny that some part of her might have preferred not to remember.

It made no difference: Takemi caught up with her on the way to school and made her remember.

"Oh, good. You're safe. Ryoko, have you seen Utsume anywhere?"

Utsume still hadn't come to school by the mid-day break.

Ryoko and Takemi had conferred for a moment and reached a conclusion: They told their story to Aki and Toshiya.

"I ran down that dark road—one of those endless roads you find in dreams—and I was panicking, like you always do in dreams. I dragged Ryoko's hand along behind me, but she was staring at nothing, like she was running unconsciously. I had no idea what to think. I was too scared to think. There was nothing I could do."

Takemi remembered a little more than Ryoko about what happened after the lights went out.

He had spent some time running down the road in total darkness. She didn't remember, but he had pulled her, dazed, along with him.

Part of her wished she could remember that. In that case, though, how had she ended up in bed? Ryoko was mystified. And the same thing had happened to Takemi.

"That's it. Next thing I knew, I was in bed. Thought it was a dream," Takemi said, pointing at his head.

Just like Ryoko, he'd been discovered asleep in bed after missing curfew. Hopefully, nobody would read too much into them both missing curfew. Ryoko flushed at the thought.

"Normally, I would say, 'It was a dream, idiot.' However . . ." Aki said, frowning. "However, since Kyo really has disappeared . . ." She sighed.

"You called him?" Toshiya asked Takemi.

"'Course, first thing. His phone was off or out of range. And, well . . . calling his house is, uh . . . you know."

"Yeah, I do," Toshiya said, nodding gravely.

Utsume's parents had split up when he was in elementary school. He lived with his father, and the two of them had been on their own ever since the divorce. But he and his father didn't get along—at all. They didn't speak to each other. When Utsume graduated college, they would have nothing to do with each other. Utsume called this their "contract."

"The moment I said what I wanted, he already was shouting. 'I don't give a damn where he sleeps!'"

"Huh. Takemi, you were pretty lucky. His dad's usually not even in the house. Sleeps at some girl's apartment."

"Really?"

"Yikes," Ryoko said, sighing. Utsume's home life always seemed so awful.

Ryoko had an older sister, and her parents both worked, so they'd managed to scrape together enough money to send both girls to school. Although Seisou Academy was expensive, they'd never balked at the price. Ryoko knew they loved her. They might fight sometimes, but they had a good relationship.

"It's just the way things are. I don't mind. Were it not for laws, parents and children would be strangers. He says I'm a parasite, using the law to siphon money away from him," Utsume had said when the subject came up.

"That's pretty harsh." Ryoko had said.

Utsume had replied, "It's a practical way of looking at it, once you take out the emotions. In that respect, I agree with his views."

It made Ryoko realize she might be really fortunate.

"If his father said that, it means Kyo wasn't home," Aki said. "I'm now sixty percent certain that Kyo vanished. The only other possibility is that he spent the night at his girlfriend's house; if we're to believe you two, though, that would be dangerous on a Peony Lantern level . . . unless you experienced some sort of group hysteria, shared the same vision . . ."

"It really happened. Trust me," Takemi said, pleading.

"Really, Aki." Ryoko affirmed, although she knew this was not the most convincing thing to do.

"I believe you," Toshiya said suddenly.

"Eh?"

"I thought something like this might happen someday. I'm not at all surprised that it finally has."

There was a unsettling silence. Toshiya's tone had been so heavy, so certain. None of them could brush it off.

Might happen someday? Ryoko wasn't sure what to make of this.

Toshiya offered no explanation. He simply said, "Utsume's my friend. I'll do something. This probably will be extremely dangerous, so you should keep your distance. Let me handle it."

There was a resolution in his eyes that left Ryoko unable to argue.

"Don't be selfish," Aki snapped, frowning irritably. "I'm not saying they're lying. I just think it's too early to make a fuss while there's still the possibility that we're wrong. It's dangerous, so we should stay away? Idiot. You think you're the only one who has the right to call yourself Kyo's friend? You're sorely mistaken," she said forcefully, staring Toshiya in the eye. Toshiya had made her mad.

This gave Ryoko enough time to recover.

"I'm His Majesty's friend, too, Murakami!"

"Right, Murakami. You can't tell us not to get involved. We already are," Takemi agreed.

"Sorry," Toshiya said, folding instantly.

"Your proposal has been rejected," Aki said, sitting back on her chair, which creaked. "How about we start with you telling us everything you know."

Four

"Let us assume that Kyo was captivated by something like a ghost and has vanished because of it. Is that correct, Murakami?" Aki asked, as though she was questioning a witness.

"Yeah, I'm sure of it."

"And you were aware that something like this might happen to him. Why?"

"Did you know Utsume has a sixth sense? He met a ghost when he was little. First grade. He's had it ever since. After that experience, Utsume always has had a powerful . . . *sympathy* toward death. His mind isn't concerned with reality. He doesn't value his own life at all. His fascination with the occult is simply one sign of his preoccupation with death."

This was pretty out there. He was talking about Utsume, though; so, for some reason, it all made perfect sense to Ryoko. Judging from the grave expression on his face, Takemi felt the same.

So, Utsume had a surprising past and mental state. Ryoko listened, feeling strange.

Toshiya continued, "He wants to die—or at least, he wants to meet a ghost again. And when he meets that ghost, he wants to follow it to the land of the dead."

"You mean, he's suicidal?"

"Not consciously. He hasn't realized any of this. He doesn't know his mind is drawn relentlessly toward death." Toshiya paused. "When I was a kid, I made a vow not to let him be killed." He was deadly serious.

Ryoko couldn't talk.

Aki asked, "You're sure it was a ghost he met?"

"Probably."

"Liar," she declared.

"Eh? What? Aki . . ."

"What do you mean?"

"Kyo met a *kami-kakushi*, right?"

"How did you . . . ?" Toshiya stammered.

Aki snorted. "It seems Murakami stubbornly refuses to provide us with important information, but he is under the mistaken impression that he is the only one who knows anything about Kyo. Take a look at this," she said, producing two photocopied pages. Each was from a page of a book, with the title and author's name written on them in Aki's handwriting.

"This incident occurred in a small village near *****, long ago.

The village children all were playing tag together when they realized that one boy was missing.

When he failed to return by nightfall, the adults searched the mountains, rivers, and the town—but they were unable to find him anywhere.

Some of the children he'd been playing with claimed to have seen him run off with a child they'd never seen previously.

Nobody in the village knew who that child was.

One year passed, then two, but the boy never returned.

Rumors spread through the village that the strange child had been a kami-kakushi."

— from ***** Prefecture Legends by the ***** Prefecture Council for Folktale Preservation

"*This is a story I heard from T, whom I met at work.*

When he was a student, T and three of his friends picked up a group of four girls.

They went to karaoke, drank a little, and—as they had intended—split up into four couples. Each couple headed off for a little private fun.

But from that day on, one of them, M, dropped out of sight.

Apparently, he never came home after that night.

His cell phone was out of range. A few days later, they filed a missing person's report.

M was last seen with a long-haired girl; when the other girls were asked about her, they insisted they didn't know her. They'd believed her to be a member of T's party.

They never figured out who the long-haired girl was.

M is still missing."

— *Oosako Eiichirou*, Modern Urban Legends

"What is . . . ?" Takemi began to ask when he'd finished reading.

"Very similar, isn't it?"

"To what's happening now? Yeah, it resembles it. Not in every way, though. From these alone—"

"True," Aki cut in, agreeing, "except these are from Kyo's books. He'd bookmarked both pages. When I borrowed them, I made copies of anything that looked interesting."

"Even so . . ."

"Obviously, that isn't all. He also loaned me a book called *On Kami-kakushi*, by the same author as those two, Oosako Eiichirou. He'd clearly read it many, many times." Aki looked at Toshiya intently. "'You interested in kami-kakushi?' I asked him. Kyo answered, 'I met one a long time ago.' It seemed to me that he wanted to encounter one again, and he was looking for them."

"Not fair."

"Sorry. Really. I wasn't sure until a minute ago. If you hadn't said that bit about thinking something like this was going to happen, I would've dismissed the possibility. I'd assumed Kyo was joking."

"*Now* will you tell us what you know?"

"Okay. Sorry, I may have underestimated you," Toshiya said decisively, bowing his head at his friends.

Ryoko and Takemi glanced at each other. The discussion was out of their league. Possibly, Toshiya had been right about them. All they could do was watch the show.

Aki glanced over at them and said, "Hey! Don't just stare. You're the ones who saw what she was, the only people who can say anything for certain."

"Uh, oh, right . . . yeah," Takemi said, perking up a little. He was easy that way.

Ryoko giggled at this.

"From what you saw, she's definitely dangerous?"

"Yeah, looked like," Ryoko nodded.

Utsume couldn't go home, Ayame had said—like a song, like a spell.

"A song? I don't like the sound of that. Someone told me that songs, poems, and spells are fundamentally the same thing."

"Ah, that was the Dark Prince!"

"And you're sure she said she'd taken Kyo?"

"It was just like Botan Dourou. No mistake about it," Ryoko said confidently; though she wasn't really sure what Botan Dourou was, only she could testify to this.

She could remember the words to the song almost perfectly.

Takemi, however, remembered next to nothing. All he could say was that it had been creepy and weird.

They'd focused on different things—just like he remembered what happened after the lights went out.

"She took him. That can mean so many things: killed him, kidnapped him, or literally took him with her. She could be a ghost, a kami-kakushi, even Red Mantle."

"More like the Leanan sídhe."

"The Leanan sídhe?"

"Fairy lover. The man they attach themselves to gains a sixth sense and becomes very successful as an artist, but they suck away his sanity, and he dies young. I'm sure Utsume told me about them."

"That fits . . ." Ryoko said, scrunching up her face. Something about the story appealed to her, and she was trying to suppress a smile. It seemed so perfect for Utsume. She couldn't stop herself from giving half a grin.

"Not really," Toshiya said, listening intently. "I think we can safely go with kami-kakushi."

Aki thought a moment before asking, "Why?"

"His mind isn't weak enough to be captivated by anything. We should assume he was walking with her of his own free will."

"Sure you aren't overestimating him?" Aki said skeptically. "We might call him the Prince of Darkness, but Kyo is human—

and up against what we believe to be a real monster. He might have met his match."

Ryoko nodded.

But Toshiya said firmly, "This has happened before."

This silenced Aki.

"He didn't just encounter a kami-kakushi. He almost was captured by one. Someone else actually was taken and has been missing for ten years now. Utsume came back . . . half alive. Ever since, Utsume's mind has been preoccupied with death. I'm absolutely certain he put himself in that monster's clutches of his own free will. However, there's no reason for him to do that with anything but a kami-kakushi. Utsume called her his 'girlfriend' because he knew exactly what she was, which explains why he suddenly told everyone he had a girlfriend: He's using her to cross over. He went with her, knowing it was suicide. Utsume sees her as a valuable foothold on the path to the other side, which he has found at last." Toshiya said. Then, he frowned.

"What's wrong?"

"Mm? Oh, it just occurred to me: Everything Kidono knows about kami-kakushi is from Utsume's books, and Takemi's thing about the Leanan sídhe was from him, as well. Even if we put our heads together, we'll never know as much about this sort of thing as Utsume does. And if he's trying to cross over . . . there might not be anything we can do."

"Ack!"

"Murakami," Aki said reproachfully. "We know that. We have to try, anyway. Don't waste thoughts. We have no time for pessimism. Never voice it again—you understand?"

"I hear you."

"Okay. Then, let me ask: Do you have an idea for how to deal with this?"

"It's not certain, but . . . yes."

"Good, then we should split up and try to do what we can. If one of us finds something, he or she immediately should call the others. Then, we move. Considering safety as well as effectively gathering information, we should work in groups of two. Murakami, especially—don't do anything on your own. You don't even have a cell phone. Understand? Good. Briefing concluded!" Aki said, ending the meeting with a flurry of orders. It was clear she was trying to prevent Toshiya from arguing.

Ryoko was grateful. She never could have done the same.

"I'm a little surprised," Takemi said. "I thought you'd say something a little more . . . harsh, Kidono. 'He's not a child, let him look after himself,' or something. I didn't think you'd be trying to save him. I guess I was wrong."

"You often are," Aki said, grimacing. "How could I sleep knowing I'd left him in mortal danger?"

Takemi gulped. "In mortal danger?"

"Of course. If he were going to wander back in a few days, it wouldn't be a kami-kakushi. There are several legends of that type where the taken do make it back; those are recorded only because they're so unusual, though. Most cases are doomed, to be frank. If it weren't Kyo, I'd already have given up. Even this century, you can find newspaper headlines on disappearances, asking if it was a kami-kakushi."

"You mean the Meiji era or Taisho?"

"Even early Showa . . . anytime someone vanishes abruptly."

Takemi swallowed. "S-so, in those cases, what happened?"

"As far as I know, nothing good."

"Ack . . ."

"At best, they found the body somewhere. Most were never seen again. Of course, I learned all this from Kyo's library. If he's doing this in full knowledge of the danger, then he's an idiot, too," Aki shrugged.

Takemi turned pale despite himself. "I w-went after something l-like that? I'm lucky to be alive!"

"Yeah," Ryoko said, suddenly realizing the things that had attacked them last night were kami-kakushi, as well. "Wow. How did we get home? Why did they let us go?"

Takemi looked puzzled. "Let us go?"

"Well, yeah. If they're as strong as that, they could've taken us easily. I don't think we got away; I think they *let* us get away."

"Huh. Why?"

"Um . . . to let us known they mean business?" Even as she said it, she wished she hadn't.

There was a long, strained silence.

Hesitantly, she asked, "Am I right?"

"Hm. I can't think of anything else," Aki nodded. "Kyo does have the worst taste in women—but even if the accident was the driver's fault, you'd still try to save him. Worry about the cause once you have. If he doesn't live through it, there's no use blaming anyone," she said casually.

"Aki, I can't tell if you're being nice or mean," Ryoko muttered.

"That's just how the world works."

"Mm." In Ryoko's eyes, Aki's social skills were a little rough. "If we're going to blame the Dark Prince, how can he make up for it?"

Aki frowned. "I don't know. If he feels guilty about making us worry, he can buy us a soda sometime. And if he thinks we made a big fuss over nothing, then we forget the whole matter."

"Because he's the victim?"

"Right, victims are hardly in a place to take responsibility for anything. It all comes down to how he feels. If all this was a conscious choice on his part, though, we might have to make him do something. . . ."

"Buy us soda?"

"Right."

Ryoko giggled. Then, a thought struck her. "What will we do to Ayame?"

As if this was the dumbest thing she'd heard all day, Aki snapped, "Make her go away. All romance between ghosts and humans ends with one or the other losing."

Ryoko bowed her head. Aki's answer struck her as heartless somehow.

"What? Ryoko, what's that look for?" Aki asked, puzzled.

"Eh?" Ryoko said, flustered. The strange feelings battling inside had shown on her face. She had no choice but to admit it. "Just . . . make her go away. I don't know, it seemed kind of sad."

"Sympathy?" Aki sighed. "That's so like you, Ryoko. If we don't do something, Kyo will never return. I understand feeling sorry for her, considering you met and talked to her; but if we aren't merciless, we might never get him back. I mean it: We can't afford to hesitate."

"Yeah, I know. Is Ayame really that bad?"

"That bad? How can you—"

"I know, I know! Still . . . how can I put this? Something about her expression . . ."

"Her expression?"

"Eh? Oh, um . . . no, never mind."

"Okay," Aki said, giving up.

Ryoko said nothing more. But she thought to herself . . . about Ayame's face when the lights went out . . . the expression she'd glimpsed when she looked up . . .

About to cry,

About to beg,

So empty,

So sad.

At the same time, there was a powerful light in her eyes, a twitch at the sides of her mouth, like she was suppressing a grin.

Which was it? Sad and lonely? Ready to give up, to beg? Miserable, resolved, hopeful, empty . . . ? What had it been? That strange face, like a martyr's . . .

"What was it?" Ryoko whispered to herself.

Chapter 3:

Thus Spoke the Night Magician

One

From the moment he laid eyes on her, he knew she was trouble: With Ayame standing next to him, Utsume's aura was scattered, shredded.

Toshiya knew how Utsume was supposed to be. Utsume's presence was so powerful—and Toshiya had known him so long—that Toshiya could sense immediately when Utsume was standing beside him.

In the ten years they'd know each other, Toshiya never once had seen Utsume so weak; it was unlikely that anyone else would understand quite how unnatural a state this was for Ustume to be in, however.

When someone with a strong aura stands near someone weaker, the weaker person is overshadowed. The reverse was unthinkable. Utsume's aura was powerful, whereas Ayame's was weak. And yet, the impossible had happened: She was feeding on his aura.

No *human* had an aura with a negative charge, though.

These were Toshiya's thoughts as he walked through the school.

He had known this would happen. He also knew whom to talk to; he'd had his eye on her, just in case. He and Takemi were headed for her now.

Truth be told, Toshiya saw no reason to follow Aki's instructions. Aki had ended the conversation, refusing to listen to arguments, but she knew full well she could not make him obey her.

He had asked Takemi along because Aki had been right when she'd said Toshiya wasn't the only one who had a right to call himself Utsume's friend. Regardless, Toshiya had no intention of involving Takemi if things got dangerous. To Toshiya, putting his friends in danger was akin to trauma—something to be avoided at all costs.

Toshiya and Utsume both were born in Hazama, and they had met in preschool.

At first, they had almost no contact with each other. Toshiya honestly couldn't remember what Utsume was like then. He might not have known Utsume's name even.

Toshiya was an odd child who had no friends. His impression was that Utsume had been an ordinary, introverted boy. It wasn't until after a certain incident happened—a kidnapping—that Toshiya first noticed him.

Toshiya heard about the case after the fact: Kyoichi Utsume was five years old at the time, when he and his three-year-old brother, Souji, abruptly vanished one day. A week later, Kyoichi came home alone, in a weakened state.

"We were blindfolded, and someone pulled our hands. We walked a long time. Souji was taken off somewhere where there were a lot of people," Kyoichi had explained.

Everyone around was terrified of the kidnappers, but there was never a ransom demand or any other sign of Souji. Eventually, the incident was recorded as a missing persons case and forgotten. Souji never came home.

After the police investigation had gone on for a while and it showed no signs of progress, a rumor began to spread through the neighborhood: kami-kakushi.

That was the first time Toshiya had heard the word. It was a simple link between a folk legend and the matter at hand, and it made Souji's situation seem more desperate. It was merely a rumor, and one that didn't help anything at all.

Eventually, the investigation was abandoned, and the case, the rumors, the legend—and Souji Utsume—stopped coming up in conversation. They were forgotten, as if *they* had met with a kami-kakushi.

Utsume hadn't come to kindergarten for a while. When he did show up again, he was a different person. He had cold eyes, eyes that seemed to have seen all the evil in the world. He'd become lost in thought any spare moment he had, withdrawing into himself at any opportunity. He put a clear distance between himself and those around him, no longer playing or running with the other children. And this was all apparent in the month after the incident; in such a short time, Utsume seemed to have aged ten years.

Knowing what they did about him, most people found Utsume hard to deal with; but for some reason, Toshiya and he got along. Utsume rejected the "enforced" style of relationships that were a part of living in modern society, so both he and Toshiya pried into each other's business as little as possible. Others may have viewed it as a distant sort of friendship; however, they were the best of friends.

On one occasion, Utsume had spoken of the case. "I really did meet a kami-kakushi," he had said. "The kami-kakushi took Souji with it."

Toshiya hadn't had any idea how to respond.

"It didn't take me—even though I wanted to go with Souji . . . to the other side."

Toshiya did not reply, so Utsume continued: "It was a real kami-kakushi. When I said that, Mommy hit me. So, I don't talk about it anymore."

When Toshiya finally learned about Utsume's family, it was already a disaster: His parents' relationship was on the decline, and the incident tore them still farther apart. His mother always had been a little prone to hysteria, and she was becoming more and more unbalanced.

Every time his parents saw each other, they would start a screaming match. To avoid it, Ustume's father headed straight into the arms of a lover he'd been seeing for years, which only served to exacerbate his wife's mental state.

The situation grew worse when the neighborhood gossip fed her depression, driving Utsume's mother into a corner. With no way to vent, she turned her hatred toward Utsume, and she began to look at him as if he were some sort of devil. Occasionally, something would set her off, and she would attack him. She didn't even care if Toshiya were watching. Half insane, she would shout, "You killed Souji, didn't you?! Everyone liked him better than you! You hated him! You killed him!"

Toshiya did not try to save Utsume or to comfort him. Utsume did not want him to. It would have been an insult to their strength. This was the kind of friendship they had.

When Utsume started elementary school, his parents got divorced. Utsume was placed in his father's care. His father despised him, as well, but his mother had been pronounced incapable of childrearing, economically and mentally.

Toshiya and Utsume attended the same elementary school. Now, in high school, Toshiya was known for his physical strength and Utsume for his frailty—but even back then, Toshiya was strong, Utsume weak. And yet, there was no sense of inequality between them.

Although children at that age tend to equate physical strength with leadership, Toshiya showed no signs of bossing anyone around, despite being the strongest in his class. Toshiya had been learning karate from his uncle since the age of three, and he constantly had been cautioned not to use strength in that way.

"If we respect the strongest, then we would have to respect the bomb. True strength comes not from the body but from the heart."

Practicing karate was simply a way to make the heart stronger, his uncle and teacher always said. Physical strength gave confidence, and confidence was the fastest way toward inner strength.

"So, we should respect good people?" Toshiya had asked.

His uncle shook his head. "No, not at all. Good, bad, normal, anyone can deserve respect. But . . ."

"But?"

"Good people are cool."

"That's lame."

He'd been punched. After that, Toshiya decided to become normal and respect-worthy. He swore off violence, not because he wanted respect but because he couldn't be bothered to fight. He had no intention of being good, and he never would've fought to defend anyone else.

"That sounds fine," his uncle had said. "Kind of a harsh world view for a kid, though."

He didn't break his vow until third grade. At the time, Utsume was being bullied, naturally.

Utsume's personality already was almost fully formed. He read a lot of books, and he couldn't fight at all. Even Toshiya thought he looked like a perfect target. To put it bluntly, Utsume was stuck up; Toshiya was, too, but his size silenced everyone. Utsume being weak, he was the one the bullies selected.

Large, rough boys surrounded him, shoving him, doing cruel things to him, laughing. Utsume never fought back, never yielded to them. He considered himself above them. No matter what they did, he ignored it. They struck him and made fun of him, but he never said anything, simply gazing back at them, ignoring them, as though nothing had happened.

This made the situation worse, and the bullying escalated. Still, Utsume never flinched; he refused to admit they were worth his time.

Utsume was strong. Having once accepted death, Kyoichi Utsume feared nothing.

And because he understood that, Toshiya did not help Utsume. It was not a heartless act, rather the result of a natural understanding that had sprung up between them. Toshiya and Utsume had been this way all along.

Until one day, when Toshiya's feelings were shaken. The leader of the bullies, a particularly rough boy, shoved Utsume. This happened all the time, but that day was particularly bad because Utsume's cold gaze had made the leader lose his temper. The leader punched him two or three times; when Utsume would only glare back at him silently, the bully lost it: He grabbed a chair and used it to hit Utsume in the head.

It was over in a second's time, and the injury was serious. Utsume's skull was fractured, and he floated between life and death for a week.

It was so horrible that Toshiya still could remember the shock: Seeing Utsume lying on the floor, a sea of blood spreading out around his head, Toshiya suddenly realized that humans easily could die if they weren't protected—just like that.

Utsume was strong, but his life was a fragile as glass. That realization drove Toshiya to his feet. He beat the leader until the bully stopped moving. Toshiya knocked him over, slammed his knees into his chest, and punched him in the face.

He knew Utsume did not want his help, did not want revenge, but Toshiya couldn't stop hitting the idiot. He had broken his own vow. And so he beat his own mistake; he beat the boy to make himself feel better.

Toshiya punched him and punched him. And then, when he saw the other boy sobbing, bent over, Toshiya stopped. The whole thing was so pointless.

The idiot had made him lose control. He felt empty inside as a result. He understood why Utsume had refused to give the bully the time of day, even when that decision essentially had been tantamount to suicide.

It was horrible: Even an idiot like this could kill someone a great as Utsume. It saddened Toshiya. Death was so . . .

After that, Toshiya believed his strength to be inferior to Utsume's.

Two

"One day, Utsume started wearing nothing but black. I asked why, and he said, 'I learned that black was the color of mourning.' He's still mourning his brother. He still wants to cross over. He has a subconscious desire to be killed. As long as Souji, his own flesh and blood, is over there, we can't stop Utsume's preoccupation with death. Nobody can."

Toshiya explained this to Takemi as they walked. He told Takemi all about Utsume and himself. He felt it was necessary.

If Aki heard this, she angrily would accuse him of arrogance: But if Toshiya failed, then Utsume—and possibly, Toshiya—would be gone forever. If that were the case, Toshiya wanted the people Utsume had called his friends to remember.

Remember Utsume.

If he told them, they'd be furious—and Utsume would be, as well. Toshiya himself knew it was arrogant, but he'd made a vow to protect his friends. Utsume, Takemi, Aki, and Ryoko . . . Toshiya was not about to let any of them die.

"Murakami, where exactly is this person?" Takemi asked, looking unusually grim. Toshiya's speech had overwhelmed him.

Striding down the school corridor, Toshiya answered, "By the pond, near the old building. She's always there."

"You mean, the witch?"

"Yeah."

"Seriously?"

Like the buildings, this school seemed to attract unusual people. When enough of them came together, a few among them grew famous for being particularly unusual. Toshiya's "help" was one such person.

A third year girl, Yomiko Togano had a reputation for being incredibly mysterious.

"Togano!" Toshiya called.

Backed by hills, there was a pond with so many lotus that it seemed almost sinister. Yomiko always stood next to that pond.

Brown streaked hair hung down to her shoulders; along with her disheveled denim jacket, this made her look normal enough, like any other girl.

She was gazing absently up at the sky. She did this any spare moment she had, occasionally smiling at nothing in particular—the first sign of how strange she was.

Yomiko heard Toshiya's call. She turned her distinctive big round eyes toward them, grinning. "There you are, Schäferhund. How unusual to see you with an ordinary person instead of the Shadow."

Takemi looked at Toshiya with as dubious an expression as he could muster.

Toshiya ignored him, saying to Yomiko, "We need your help."

Yomiko nodded, looking very interested.

When Toshiya had finished, Yomiko said, "How horrible," in a tone of voice that suggested it wasn't horrible at all. She grinned.

Toshiya had explained things in worrying detail. "You sure she's okay?" Takemi asked, but Toshiya just nodded. She was the only person he knew with any kind of sixth sense.

Yomiko was the real thing. Utsume had said so. Last year, when he and Toshiya had first met Yomiko here, she was staring at the sky.

Utsume had said, "Can you see? I can only smell."

Yomiko had turned to them with a huge smile. "I can. You're the Shadow, aren't you? And the one behind you is Schäferhund, who used to be a wolf."

"Schäferhund?"

"Or 'German Shepherd,' if you prefer. It sounds better in German, doesn't it?"

He had no idea what she was talking about. Afterward, however, he heard a lot of people talking about Yomiko—the mysterious Yomiko Togano.

"Eccentric? Crazy? No, she's really psychic!" People said all kinds of things. Some said she'd spent some time in an asylum, whereas others claimed she had introduced them to a medium.

"Probably true," Utsume had said.

"Which part?"

"That she has paranormal abilities—not exactly psychic, but she does have the sight. And there's a good chance that someone more powerful is behind her," he said. "There's a scent on her that isn't hers."

Toshiya didn't know why, but from that moment on, he had kept Yomiko in mind as an advisor in case anything should happen. He continued to meet her every now and then, keeping in contact.

And today, he knew his efforts had not been in vain.

"I've seen that girl," Yomiko said after they described Ayame.

Toshiya and Takemi's expressions changed.

"Where?"

"At school. She was always here, chanting beautiful songs. I guess no one else saw her, though."

"Yet you did?" Takemi asked.

"Sure," Yomiko grinned. "Because I'm a witch."

It wasn't clear whether Yomiko was aware of it, but the main reason people thought she was crazy was that she always called herself a witch. People believed in psychics, but nobody believed in witches. Still, Yomiko insisted on calling herself one.

"I can't use magic, I don't fly around on a broomstick, and I can't talk to black cats. Even so, I'm a witch."

She was mysterious. Mysterious girls often are accepted if they're cute; however, her witch declaration kept people away. Still, no matter what anyone said to her, she kept introducing herself that way.

Her behavior was consistently odd, enough to give her the reputation of "she's a little weird."

Toshiya didn't care. None of that had anything to do with her ability.

"What can we do to get Utsume back?" he asked.

Yomiko cocked her head. "Good question. I don't know."

Toshiya looked crestfallen. "You don't?"

"I know someone who might, though."

"Will you tell us who?" Toshiya said, leaning forward.

"That depends on the strength of your desire," Yomiko said, giggling as she fended him off.

"What do you mean?"

"Exactly as I said. This friend of mine is a little unusual. He can do anything. If your desire lacks strength, though, he won't help you."

At first, he'd thought she wanted something in return. However, it seemed that wasn't the case.

Yomiko continued, "He is the most powerful psychic, seer, and magician I know. He is very good with magic, but he has grown too close to the secrets of magic, becoming magic itself. There is no longer anything limiting his power; however, he himself has lost all desire. Magic is the power to make people's desires come true; magic itself wants nothing. So, he makes people's desires come true."

Toshiya understood none of this.

Yomiko smiled. "Okay, I'll introduce you. If your desire is genuine, he will help you. That's what he does. Wait a moment."

As Toshiya and Takemi stood confused, Yomiko took a cell phone from her pocket. She pulled out the antenna, and the phone *suddenly rang*. She answered, saying, "Yes, Jinno? Got a favor. Yeah, okay. That shop?"

Toshiya gulped. Something was very wrong.

"Wh-what just happened?" Takemi whispered.

Toshiya couldn't answer.

"Thank you," Yomiko said, ignoring them and hanging up.

She put the phone back in her pocket, and then she took out a box of matches—a thick, old-fashioned box from a coffee shop.

"Okay, he'll meet you. This shop, whenever you like."

Toshiya took half a step backward. He had sharp ears and could hear the receiver: The only sound coming from it was the high-pitched whine of a fax machine or modem.

Yomiko held out the matches.

When Toshiya stood there, dumbfounded, she grinned.

$$\bigcirc \quad \bigcirc \quad \bigcirc$$

Three

The coffee shop, Mu Myo An, meaning "restaurant with no name," was on a back road behind a row of office buildings some distance from Hazama station.

Following the map on the back of the matches, they turned the corner past the dilapidated office buildings. There, they found an alley lined with back entrances—the shop's elegant exterior was the one bright spot in the general dinginess.

There were no customers.

When they opened the door, a chime rang.

"Welcome," the shop owner's deep voice said.

"Two coffees."

The owner nodded, and he silently began getting them ready.

Toshiya and Takemi sat down. It wasn't the friendliest shop, but the atmosphere wasn't bad. It did seem a little somber, but that might've been their imagination.

Quiet music played in the background. It was an old record, and the scratches almost blotted out the melody. What was presumably a viola played a piece they'd never heard previously. If they listened closely, they could tell the player was bowing with exceptional ferocity; however, between the record's condition and the low volume, the original piece's power was lost.

Toshiya stopped listening. The melody struck him as being incredibly ominous.

"Is he really coming?" Takemi asked.

"I guess," Toshiya answered.

It was after school on the same day that Yomiko had given them the matches. Yomiko had specified the place, telling them the time was up to them. Toshiya had tried to estimate how long it would take them to get there to give her a time.

"Oh, don't worry. Just show up. Time has no real meaning for him." Yomiko ultimately refused to specify a time.

It had taken a while to find the shop. It was now past six and, outside of themselves, no one knew they were in the shop.

"It's not gonna turn out the shop owner is the magician, is it?"

"It would be awfully rude to ask." Toshiya said, although it did make sense. In an out-of-the-way place like this, with no customers . . . the shop wouldn't seem to be very successful. If the shop owner was really the magician, and the shop was just a front, it would explain everything.

"Here you are," the master said, placing their coffee on the table. Dark ripples spread on the surface of the liquid.

The shop owner returned to the counter without another word.

Guess not, Toshiya thought—and the music was drowned out by a horrible screech, which hurt their ears. The needle had slid right off.

"Whoops," the owner said, standing up.

Both Toshiya and Takemi turned toward him.

"Let us speak of illusion, desire, and fate."

Takemi jerked back in his chair so hard he almost went over backward.

Toshiya's heart was in his mouth. The voice had come from right in front of him: There was a man in black sitting across from Toshiya, next to Takemi.

They had looked away, turning toward the counter for a split second. In that instant, he had appeared in their blind spot—without a sound.

The man had long black hair, pale skin, and long, thin, black eyes, which peered through tiny round glasses. His body was wrapped in an incredibly long black coat; because he was sitting down, it was hard to tell—it might've been a cape. Either way, his clothing looked as if it were from a movie set in the Meiji or Taisho era. Around the collar of his white shirt, he wore a black string in place of a necktie.

The man smiled. His thin lips turned up on both sides, twisting into a mocking grin, like he was terribly, horribly amused.

He resembled Utsume somehow. Not only his presence, something about his essence . . . the darkness in his heart. The atmosphere he carried with him froze the hearts of those who saw him.

Utsume, however, never smiled.

Toshiya stared at the man's smile as one would an unsettling sculpture.

"Are you . . . Jinno?"

"Indeed, I am Jinno Kageyuki, a magician, or what you might call a 'psychic,'" he replied. Then, Jinno abruptly asked, "Do you two believe in supernatural phenomenon? Or not?"

Toshiya and Takemi looked at each other.

"Um . . ." Takemi managed, trying to say something.

Before he could, Toshiya said, "Neither."

Toshiya believed it was his job to save Utsume; if so, he had to take the initiative here.

Takemi swallowed his words.

Jinno's eyes crinkled. "Mm, wise answer. Very sensible. Have you ever felt that the world revolved around two things alone—namely, beginnings and endings?"

"Too poetic for me to understand."

"Clearly. You have the makings of a fine warrior, not a good hunter. A hunter would have said, 'No. Beginnings and endings are the same thing,'" Jinno chuckled.

Takemi's face registered incomprehension.

Toshiya felt the same but ignored that feeling. The conversation had only just begun. "I don't care either way. I simply want to know how to save Utsume."

"Certainly. Then, let us stop discussing fate and proceed to illusion," Jinno said, folding his arms on the table and resting his chin on one hand.

"Illusion?"

"Yes, illusion. I'm afraid we won't be discussing desire. I did not show myself because of your desire, rather because I was interested in your fate."

"Does that mean you can't help?" Toshiya sighed.

Jinno shook his head. "You need knowledge. Knowledge is the one weapon, the one method we have of affecting destiny. I have an interest in your story: I'm curious to know what you will make of your destiny. You want to know how, and I can tell you, because I want to see what resolution you will bring to the matter of the boy you call the Dark Prince and the girl you call kami-kakushi, as well as all the destinies connected to them."

Toshiya frowned. They had not explained anything to Jinno; how did he know about Utsume and Ayame?

"Did you hear about them from Togano?" he asked.

Jinno didn't answer. Instead, he began talking quietly, "So, let us talk about illusion. Were you aware that the other side has been invading this world for a long time? Heh heh, no need to look so displeased. I used a simplified expression, but you don't like the word 'invade,' hm? It does sound a bit like a third-rate novel, doesn't it? To be more strictly accurate, we could use words like 'assimilate,' 'merge,' or 'encroach.' In truth, this is their nature; they have no real will to 'invade,' per se."

The conversation had taken an absurd turn. Even prior to that, however, Toshiya found himself shuddering.

Jinno's voice and words had an unpleasant, slimy feel to them, as if he was reciting some forbidden spell. And his voice had a horrible sweetness—like syrup. Like poison.

"This other world is right next to our own, and that world always has been connected to our own," Jinno gave an oily chuckle. "This is what I meant by 'invade.' Nobody knows, nobody notices, but our world steadily is being eaten by the other world, as you already have experienced," he said, glancing at Takemi. "Mankind has been fighting with them since the dawn of time. Do you believe me?"

Takemi met Jinno's gaze and gulped. Jinno's eyes seemed to suck him in, and Takemi's expression registered all the anxiety and fear filling him. Finally, Takemi broke eye contact, looking for help.

Toshiya glared at Jinno. From Jinno's expression, he couldn't tell if all this had been a lie, a joke, a delusion, or the truth.

"So, you can't believe me," Jinno said, meeting Toshiya's gaze. "You don't need to. I do not demand faith, devotion, or anything like it. The word 'psychic' is your term; to be accurate, I am not a psychic. This is not my occupation . . . I simply explain, as I have been for quite a long time. Will you listen?" he asked, as if well aware that he seemed unreliable.

Toshiya had no choice but to nod.

"Then, I will continue," Jinno said, nodding back. "We don't know why they—the beings from this other world—are trying to cross over to ours. They might have a reason, or they might not. Their very existence is beyond human understanding. They are fundamentally different from mankind, existing in a higher dimension; although

they are always near us, most humans are unable to sense them, in the same way that higher mathematical equations are nothing but a meaningless row of symbols to people who haven't studied them. It's exactly the same. We all are looking at the same thing, yet only a few select humans will be able to pick them out from the background. They can understand the meaning of the equation. That's how few people can see them. And when they can . . . that ability is what you call a 'sixth sense.' The ability to comprehend uncanny beings; well, only people with limitless imagination can see them. This aptitude can be rather unfortunate, as you well know."

"So, are you . . . one of these unfortunate people?"

"Heh heh. Maybe, maybe not. At any rate, normal humans are unable to detect them. The odd thing is, they never lay a finger on anyone that can't. We don't know if they have some sort of rule, or if they are trying to get us to understand them—or perhaps, they simply *can't*. We don't know the reason, but we do know they are unable to attack someone incapable of detecting them. So, that is where their 'invasion' begins.

"There are many methods they can use. Let me give you two examples: The first one, we call 'fablization'; the second, 'assimilation.' Both are classic examples of their methods," Jinno said, raising his index finger and twirling it in the air theatrically.

Four

"Human beings are a fascinating life form. I mean, they are fully capable of taking something they cannot see—or even prove the existence of—and processing it until it becomes common knowledge," Jinno said, folding his arms on the table again.

Toshiya frowned dubiously. He had no idea where this was going.

"Take, for example, the atom. It's an accepted fact that everything on Earth is made up of tiny little things called atoms. Of all the people that know this fact, though, how many actually have seen an atom with their own eyes? Have you? Have you seen an atom? Of course not. They're unimaginably small. Regardless, you accept that everything is made up of them.

Or take the universe. The universe is expanding. However, there are only a few places in the world capable of observing the expansion of the universe. Only a handful of people have seen it with their own eyes. Yet, based on the observations of that handful, it has become accepted as common sense that the universe is expanding. . . ."

"What's your point?"

"You don't know? This is what we call 'fabilization.'"

"Here's another example: What do you think of ghost stories? Ghosts, monsters, the supernatural, *youkai*, apparitions—they are called many things. All are popular examples of things that cannot be proven by science; and yet, you *know* about them. You know that kitsune and *tanuki youkai* trick humans. You know that ghosts haunt people, that monsters hurt people. You don't know if they are real; nonetheless, they are part of your common knowledge.

"They use this human tendency to enter our consciousness: By transforming into stories, they make people aware of them. The drawback to this is that they are forced to conform to the narrative of the story; however, considering that it greatly increases their pool of potential prey, it's an extremely effective method. Whereas they themselves are beyond the scope of human imagination, people can catch a glimpse of them in ghost stories and urban legends.

"Now, how about the legend of the kami-kakushi—a being that pulls people into another world before they know it; sounds like something they would like, doesn't it?"

Toshiya shivered. That meant . . . "Does that mean she's one of them?"

"In a sense. Not quite. She is a kami-kakushi; her essence and history make her different from them, though. Why? Because she is a human who was pulled into that other world.

"Fablization occurs when a sensitive's experiences are turned into words, allowing them to approach people who have some knowledge of what they are. Most ghost stories are simply stories, though, and words are much too limiting a form of expression: Words can express only a portion of a fragment of their true nature. The stories form the seed of common knowledge, but that seed isn't strong enough. So, they proceeded to the logical next step: pulling sensitives into their world and attempting to transform those sensitives into beings like themselves.

"This is what we call 'assimilation.' People suddenly vanish—or change. Assimilation is happening at the same time as fablization. And the kami-kakushi of folklore are one example of this.

"I don't know when she lived, but she was assimilated by them at some point, and only sensitives could detect her. Anyone she was with would be pulled gradually into the other world, as well—which is exactly how she got there in the first place, and how she came to be doing what she was: appearing to people capable of perceiving her, thanks to the legend of the kami-kakushi. She is both human and the same as them—capable of living only within the confines of an urban legend. Her heart is human; however, like them, she exists eternally for one sole purpose. Are you beginning to understand what she is?"

His question was met by silence. The scratchy noises from the record—sounds like flowing sand—quietly filled the shop.

"But . . ." Toshiya said. "I—we all saw her, too."

"A very good observation," Jinno said, raising his index finger. "This is why altering a human is so advantageous: Although she is one of them, she also is human. When she is with humans, she is only human. In other words, she normally is difficult to perceive; once she has met a sensitive capable of perceiving her, though, that person will transmit her, allowing her to enter other humans' consciousness. When humans meet and talk, they often feel a strange sort of mutual awareness, especially if they are close. She uses this bond between them to 'infect' them, essentially. Her signal is relayed, as it were. Her existence is like a code, and the sensitive translates that into something easier to understand. I suppose the easiest way to put it is that if you're introduced to her, you can see her. She is, after all, human, making her much easier to see than they are. This increases the number of people who can see her, spreading the legend and helping to prepare for their eventual invasion."

"I see!" Toshiya said, linking Jinno's lecture to his own feelings when he first saw Ayame.

It wasn't that he believed what the man was saying; still, so far, nothing the man said had contradicted anything Toshiya knew to be true.

Although, that would mean that the inhuman girl who made Utsume disappear . . . "That means . . . she's a victim?" Toshiya asked, glaring.

"She is both victim and assailant," Jinno's smile grew wide. "The first thing humans transformed into kami-kakushi experience is absolute isolation. They can call out, they can scream, but nobody will notice them. They find themselves suddenly not part of the world. The isolation and loneliness are so intense that they start to go mad. And then, at last, a sensitive appears, someone who can see them. Imagine the relief. And they can make contact with the people around the sensitive, as well.

"Once transformed, however, they have become monsters. They slowly draw the person they have grown closest to into the other world, regardless of what they want. There is nothing they can do to stop it. That person is swiftly sliced out of reality—and not long after, the friend they made is eaten by the other world."

"Utsume. What happens to the people that are . . . 'eaten'?"

"Many things. They might transform, as well, residing within that uncanny story. They might get lost in the madness of that other world and have their soul torn apart, being reduced to nothing. They might be trapped in the other world, wandering forever. And if they are very lucky, the two of them might remain together in the other world, living out an unchanging story. However, there is little hope of that: Once humans are pulled into that world, they either die or become monsters, without exception. The same fate awaits them all: the pain of loss and unbearable isolation. Their soul damaged once more, the kami-kakushi returns to that endless cycle of sin and isolation. This continues until they either vanish or go mad."

"Ugh." Takemi groaned, as if he couldn't stand to hear more.

Toshiya's fists tightened. "So, what? We should feel sympathy for her? Let her take Utsume?"

"Of course not," Jinno chuckled. "Did you come here just to listen to me babble this gibberish? If that were true, there would be no point in my being here. I desire nothing. I expect nothing. I merely provide knowledge, means, and temporary conflict; use them as you will. Make your own story. That is all I want from you. Even—"

Jinno stared into Toshiya's eyes. "Even if that means you must kill something else."

Then, he laughed. "But she's already a monster. It is next to impossible for a human to kill her. So, let me warn you: If a human raises a hand against a monster, it is the human who gets hurt."

Jinno laughed again. His bottomless eyes, filled with mirth, knew everything about Toshiya, whose every inch was covered in goose bumps.

This . . .

This feeling . . .

This horrible feeling . . . as though his soul were being drained away . . .

"So, let us put an end to the madman's lecture," Jinno said

The feeling dissipated just as Toshiya realized it was fear.

"Don't believe a word I said. I was, of course, joking. Forbidden knowledge and jokes are very similar in that they ultimately lead to nothing but misfortune. Occasionally, they are even the same thing.

"Now, I don't intend this as a way of thanking you for hearing me out, but I will now give you the 'method' you seek before vanishing."

87

Toshiya suddenly noticed that sweat was pouring down his own forehead. What had happened just now? He tried to hide how rattled he was. Jinno had him. He'd been lost in Jinno's words. Now, Toshiya looked at Jinno.

Jinno casually raised his right hand to eye level. "You said you want to save the vanished human. Generally speaking, if you don't want to lose something, the best method is to keep it in sight. Humans, however, have only two eyes; unlike cat's eyes, they do not see very well in the dark. So, in this case, it would be very difficult. That means . . . well, if your pet cat frequently ran off, what would you do?"

Toshiya thought for a moment. He was recovering his composure. "Put a bell on it."

"Exactly," and like magic, a bell rang in Jinno's hand. "Put a bell on it, and you will know where your lost cat is. Of course, you can't put a bell on a person until you have found that person—but this bell will lead you to him, like a charm or a signal flare. Take it."

Torn, Toshiya hesitated for a second . . .

. . . and in that moment, Takemi took the bell.

Ring. It chimed in Takemi's hand.

Apparently, Takemi had felt slightly put out that the conversation had focused on Toshiya all this time. He tossed the bell around in his hand, smiling like he'd accomplished something.

"Wait," he said, frowning. He peered inside the bell. "It won't ring! There's nothing inside! B-but, I just heard it. . . ."

"Really?"

"Really. This bell's empty," Takemi said, tilting his head, puzzled.

Jinno crinkled up his eyes. "Then, my role is done," he said, standing up. "If you find him again, do not take your eyes off him. Kami-kakushi will appear the moment you look away."

The cloak of darkness that had been wrapped around Jinno spilled to the floor: It was a cape. Utsume had said that capes were a symbol of mysticism: Inside them, secrets lurked. Seen up close, the cape's color was too complex to call black. Jinno's white hand parted the evening-shaded mantle. His hand reached out toward them.

"Remember," he said, grinning. "If you let him out of your sight—watch what happens."

The hand that was stretched out toward them turned, pointing to the side—toward the counter.

The shop owner was standing alone, his hands on the record. He turned toward them.

When he saw the two boys staring at him like they'd seen a ghost, he cocked his head, puzzled.

That was all. It was nothing.

"Nothing happened?" Toshiya said, looking back.

His jaw dropped: There was nothing there. In the moment Toshiya and Takemi had taken their eyes off him—in that instant—Jinno had vanished.

They had felt nothing, heard nothing.

Jinno should have been there, but the air sat quietly, unmoving, as if there hadn't been anyone there in the first place.

"That's what happens." Jinno's laugh, in their memories. Then, those memories, they began to fade, as well. A moment later, neither of them could remember what Jinno looked like. His voice, his appearance . . . a strong impression remained, but the details were blurred, the memories fuzzy.

The only thing left behind was the bell in Takemi's hand. It was the proof that they'd met Jinno.

"Murakami," Takemi whispered, "are we dreaming?"

Toshiya thought for a second. "No."

Chapter 4:

Thus Spoke the Magic Hunter

One

"Brrr, April's always colder than you expect," Ryoko said, pulling the collar of her spring jacket closed as she walked.

"Yeah," Aki said, keeping her hands in her pockets.

They were a short distance outside of Hazama city. Although spring, the biting wind reminded them that it could still go right through them.

Aki and Ryoko were headed to a hospital. Five past seven was well beyond the normal hospital operating hours, though. It was past dusk and heading into night, which meant it was getting darker.

Ryoko had called the dorm to tell them she would be staying the night at Aki's apartment. Once she'd given the phone to Aki, who had confirmed this information, Ryoko was given permission. She imagined other schools probably would not be quite so easy-going.

Hazama abruptly turned into country outside the confines of the city; it was marked more by fields and forests than houses, and the roads were dark. It wasn't really the kind of place for two girls to be walking alone. But it was too late to regret going by themselves.

"I didn't think it would be this late."

"Me neither."

"I hope it doesn't take all night. Thank goodness tomorrow is Saturday."

"Yeah. Sorry for dragging you along."

"Forget it! This is kind of fun."

"Really?" Aki said dubiously. She quickened her pace.

She really hadn't planned to be out so late.

After school on the same day that she'd made Toshiya promise to cooperate, she and Ryoko had headed to Shuzenji, a Shingon Buddhist temple located about ten minutes on foot from Seisou University. They both were on the same mountain, so they were neighbors. And the university was right next to the branch schools, so it was still a short walk from the high school to the temple.

The temple was not particularly old; at the earliest, it was founded during the Edo period. Aki guessed it had been founded by the shogun to keep control. Despite its origins, though, the head priest resided in the temple, making it surprisingly traditional. (It was more common these days for the priest and his family to have a house built for them to live in.)

"If you meet with something supernatural, the first place most people go is a temple or shrine, followed by an exorcist, and finally a cult of some kind. That last step is reserved for the very desperate." Aki had said. So, they had set off.

Their choice of shrine was not random, however. Apparently, *tsukimono-suji* were unusually common in the Hazama area, and it seemed all victims of it headed straight for Shuzenji.

Tsukimono-suji were, roughly, families that provided a home to some sort of spirit. It might be an *inugami* (dog god), a *sarugami* (monkey god), or a *hebigami* (snake god). If the spirit were treated well, the family would prosper; if neglected, the household would fall.

These spirits would accompany members of that bloodline around whether they were wanted or not. They would react to ill will or jealousy and, regardless of the family's personal desires, they would cause harm to any offending individual, as well as anyone connected to that individual. Rumors used to be relatively common that one family or another were tsukimono-suji. And there used to be people who would free families from those spirits' influence; in Hazama, that had been done mostly at Shuzenji.

All of which Aki had learned from Utsume, which is why she had decided to head for Shuzenji first. She was prepared to be disappointed. If all they had to offer was a sermon and a prayer, she would leave quickly.

Sure enough, when the young head priest came out to meet them, Aki instantly decided they were wasting their time: Naturally, his hair was slicked back, and a Rolex gleamed beneath the sleeve of his robes.

"Welcome," he greeted them, flashing his teeth.

Aki almost said, "Never mind," but she stopped herself. At times like this, having a sharp tongue got in her way.

The priest gave his name as Kijou; he looked less like a priest than a *yakuza* in priest's robes. When Aki explained about the girl they believed to be a ghost, though, he seemed very interested.

"Will you tell me more?" Kijou urged.

"Not if you're just curious," Aki said.

"If I were only curious, I hardly would admit it," Kijou said, laughing, dismissing her doubts.

This surprised Aki. She revised her opinion of the man. At the least, he was not an idiot, a liar, or a phony, making a pretense of kindness. More than anything else, Aki hated people who disguised their curiosity in a show of kindness; ultimately, they were completely useless.

Kijou did not deny his curiosity, and he didn't caution that he might not be able to help. His attitude was one of allowing her to talk if she wanted to. Tricky.

"Okay," Aki said, and she proceeded to explain the details to the priest. It couldn't hurt to try.

Kijou listened silently. He didn't laugh or scoff. Nor did he give his opinion or perspective. And he did not nod along and agree with her. When he did open his mouth, it was to ask for further detail—usually along the lines of, "How did you feel then?" or "Did that feel strange?" He always seemed to ask about things that really didn't have much to do with the matter at hand, as if he'd read a "how to" book on counseling.

When Ryoko told him about her experience, these questions became more obvious. He asked about every aspect of what she'd seen, about her feelings and physical reactions. He sounded more like a doctor than a priest.

When they'd finished explaining, it was already six thirty. They'd reached the temple at five thirty; so, what they'd expected to be a half hour conversation had doubled in length. Sitting properly and talking was exhausting, and Aki sighed.

Kijou brought some green tea for them. He smiled. "I have three final questions for you. Will you answer?" he said, giving them a probing look.

He was grinning, but his eyes weren't smiling at all. Aki began to wonder if this man was actually a priest.

"Yes," she said.

"First question: This . . . Utsume, was it? Do you have any idea what reason, cause, or impetus might have led to his disappearance? Any evidence or proof of it?"

Aki and Ryoko glanced at each other.

"She caused it. But we have no proof."

"No evidence, either."

"What reason would she have to take Utsume?"

"We don't know."

"What about the cause?"

"What do you mean, exactly?"

"For example, did he do something bad, leading to his being haunted? Does someone hate him enough to put a curse on him?"

"Nothing I could say for certain."

"Okay, I understand," Kijou said, glaring upward in thought. "Second question: This girl . . . had either of you heard any stories about a ghost that takes people away? Did you read about it in a book? Was there a chance that Utsume knew about it? Anything like that?"

"No rumors . . ." Aki said, trailing off. She wasn't sure if she really should tell everything. This man was too enigmatic to trust fully. She hesitated for a minute. But in the end, she told him. She'd already tasted the poison; she might as well polish the plate.

"I do know about a book, though."

"Oh?" Kijou said, impressed, as if he hadn't expected an answer. "Do you know the author and title?"

"Oosako Eiichiro's *Modern Urban Legends*."

"Oh, that's real. I'm surprised you could find it; it's extremely rare."

"You've heard of it?"

Kijou smiled vaguely. He wasn't denying it; he was being evasive. This man had not once said anything definite. However, his manner suggested that he knew something.

"Is the book yours?"

"No, it was Utsume's. I had copied the page in question."

"Only one copy?"

"Yes."

"May I borrow it?"

"Certainly."

"Then, please," he said, taking the copy and pouring them more tea. "I won't be a moment," he said. "Wait here. I still have one last question."

Kijou stood up and vanished through the sliding door.

Ryoko sipped her tea. They could smell incense in the air.

Aki perked up her ears. Kijou appeared to be making a phone call.

They sat in silence.

Kijou hung up, but he still did not return.

Ryoko whispered, "He's taking ages."

"Yeah."

"What's he doing?"

"Don't know. Be on your guard."

"Mm? Why?"

"I think he's more than a priest."

"Why? The Rolex? They all have that. The priest at my grandfather's funeral came in a Mercedes."

"Not that," Aki said, putting one hand to her temple, disgusted by Ryoko's density. "All the time he was questioning us, he was watching our expressions—and by that, I don't mean making eye contact. His eyes kept flicking back and forth between us. He was observing our reactions, like he was trying to tell if we were lying, or trying to psychoanalyze us."

"Really?"

"Yeah. He's a pro. He's practiced that until it's second nature to him. Normally, you don't see that from anyone but cops and counselors. A priest shouldn't be capable of it."

"So, you mean . . ."

"I don't know if he's real or not. He's no ordinary priest, though. If people were led to believe he was a nouveau riche who just shows up to read a sutra at a funeral, he'd knock their legs out from under them."

"Aki, maybe you should say things like that more quietly," Ryoko said, glancing nervously at the door Kijou had left through. She was worried about being overheard.

Aki listened for a moment, but she couldn't tell if he was close enough to eavesdrop.

"Yeah," she said, deciding not to worry Ryoko any more, even though she had raised her voice deliberately, figuring if he knew they were on their guard, he wouldn't try to pull anything.

Whether he'd heard or not, he came back in a few minutes later. "Sorry about that," he said, sitting down again and giving them a slightly different smile than he had before.

"As for my final question," he said. "Why did you decide to come to Shuzenji with this problem?"

Aki answered, "You have a reputation. At least until the Showa era, there are documents that mention Shuzenji fighting tsukimono-suji."

"Well now, that *is* well researched. I'm impressed," Kijou said, sounding genuine.

Aki agreed. She hadn't found the documents; Utsume had.

"Let me introduce you to Shuzenji's expert on these matters," Kijou said, reaching into the sleeve of his robe and dramatically producing something from inside.

For a moment, Aki tensed, wondering what suspicious object might emerge. It turned out to be a pair of ordinary cards on purple paper. Surprised, she said, "What are those?"

"These will take you to our expert. This incident is, in all probability, the real thing, so I'm sending you here," he said calmly.

"Now, I'm angry," Aki replied forcefully.

The cards were referral slips to a hospital. The hospital's name was The Naijin Association Foundation Hospital.

Ryoko appeared equally shocked—and naturally so: The Naijin Association Foundation Hospital was an isolated mental hospital, famous enough in the area that "you ought to go see Naijin" often was uttered as a joke.

"Let's go, Ryoko," Aki said, standing up.

Kijou hurriedly stopped them. "Oh no, you've got me wrong! Wait!"

"I can't possibly imagine any way in which I might be wrong," Aki snapped, refusing to sit down.

"I mean, please listen. The normal referral slips are green," Kijou smiled weakly. "There's an expert in this type of matter at the Naijin hospital. These purple cards will take you directly to him. Even if you don't believe me, why don't you go and see? If you have these cards, you can get in anytime, twenty-four hours a day. Of course, earlier is better—before it's too late to help Utsume."

He held out the cards again. Neither girl moved.

Kijou grimaced. "Really. It's impossible for me to trick you into going to the hospital to have you committed. They need approval from the governor to hold anyone against that person's will. Even then, they can do it only if the person is violent or dangerous. Both of you are completely sane. You'll be fine."

Aki carefully observed the priest, in the same way he'd been observing them. She intended him to notice.

He soon did.

"Oh," he said, letting his head droop, cards still held out in front of him. He clearly had no idea what to do now.

There was a long silence.

Then, Aki grinned. She snatched the cards from his hand and handed one over to Ryoko.

"Huh?"

Ryoko was taken aback by this sudden movement, as was Kijou.

Aki giggled. "Don't underestimate us just because we're in high school. Your negotiating tactics are sloppy. I'm sorry I made fun of you, but I hate being treated like an idiot."

Kijou's jaw dropped. At last, he figured out what had happened and laughed heartily along with Aki.

Meanwhile, Ryoko stood stammering, "Huh? What? Um." She looked cluelessly from one to the other.

They laughed a while longer.

Finally, Kijou said, "Not fair at all. You really had me going. I'm sorry I underestimated you." He scratched his head. "So, genius, you trusted me the whole time?"

"Not really," Aki said, shaking her head. "I have no one else to ask, though. If you can do something, then of course I'm going to see if it works."

"Very wise," Kijou grinned.

Aki did not smile back.

She already had turned her back on him and put her mind to figuring out the best way to get to the Naijin hospital.

Ryoko stood up, as well. "Straight there?" she asked, picking up her coat. It was less a question than a statement.

"Yep," Aki nodded. "We have to help Kyo."

Two

"Hey, did you see? The Dark Prince has a girlfriend!"

When she'd first heard this from Ryoko, a quiet tremor had run through Aki's heart.

"Huh?" she had replied, her voice registering total disbelief. To Aki, the voice seemed to be coming from someone else.

It wasn't disbelief. It was panic, caused by this sudden, unexpected blow to her secret love for Utsume.

Aki Kidono was unflappable. Only she knew that was solely a surface trait.

Aki Kidono had an acid tongue. Only she knew how much harm and distress she caused herself with it.

Aki Kidono was smart as a whip. Only she knew that this intelligence left a moat between her and others, building walls as she fended off everyone else.

"It boggles the mind. Kyo is basically a psychopath."

The fact that she said this to hide her affection for him was her greatest worry. She constantly kept her feelings hidden so that no one would know, least of all Utsume. Eventually, they would graduate and go their separate ways; it would all be over. That fate was approaching quickly, and the prospect terrified her. To tell him how she actually felt, though? Her pride, her reluctance to show any weakness, and her fear that he wouldn't allow her . . . her instincts to make herself look strong overrode everything else.

Aki was as strong as glass—and just as breakable.

Despite the rumors, Aki's family was not rich.

Her father might have made a little more money than the average man, but her mother was an ordinary housewife. They were a normal family.

The unusual thing about them was that both her parents were extremely intelligent: Aki's father was a researcher at an engineering firm, and he had met her mother at grad school. That was all, though.

Her older brother had inherited her parents' scientific abilities. Aki, meanwhile, read as many books as possible.

Her teachers still talk about how she read through the entire school library in three years. When there was nothing left to read at school, she began going to the public library so often that all the librarians knew her name.

Aki was quiet and smart, and she made a good impression on adults. Her teachers all adored her. The price for this was that the other students often bullied her.

Bullying is always a sinister thing. The character type of the big strong kid, with his illogical but relatively harmless bullying, doesn't exist in real life. No, the reality is much more sinister and secretive, operating largely on a system by which the bully's hand is never seen.

Girls, especially, seldom resort to violence: In elementary school, her slippers were hidden. The right one was found in the toilet, the left one in the mud—when they cleaned the ditch, two months later. Her textbooks were dunked in the toilets; and a few days later, her notebooks. A day later, her recorder met the same fate. Graffiti appeared on her backpack. She could wash off the magic marker, not the words that had been cut into it with a chisel. Aki changed backpacks five times in six years.

She never knew why.

She could no longer count the number of times or methods by which she'd been bullied. Every one of them took their toll on her heart. After six years, she entered junior high, but nothing changed.

The junior high was a little bigger than her elementary school. Most of her classmates followed her there, and the bullying got worse. Everyone ignored Aki. No matter what she did, no matter how sad she was, no matter how upset, no one paid any attention to her. They never spoke to her, never came near her. At best, they would glance at her and giggle.

Even if she went to the teachers, they couldn't do anything. The bullying was too shapeless. Everyone was a ringleader, everyone a cooperator, everyone an observer, everyone a neutral third party. Telling the teacher just made things worse.

At first, she cried. The pain, the suffering, the misery, the anger, the powerlessness, the unfairness—it overwhelmed her, and she cried. Crying just made them laugh louder, though. And when she realized that, she stopped crying.

Contempt replaced her tears. A warped pride supported her. She looked down on all of them, despising their stupidity and internally mocking all her classmates, who all were part of the bullying system.

She was special; that's why she was persecuted. She shored up her ego with thoughts like these, and she was able to bear the continued bullying. Fools were foolish and did foolish things. She did not. Was that not proof of her mental superiority? To her, this was Truth. At the same time, she knew this was warped thinking.

The strength she gained by looking down on other people prevented her from getting close to them. She knew full well that would do nothing to improve her current situation. She was objective and smart enough to figure out that much. And yet, she wasn't about to stop. If she stopped, she would shatter. Once a system was made, once a label given, it was not easy to change. If Aki had chosen to do anything but stand her ground, the unchanging situation would have led her to despair. Dramatic changes do not happen in the real world.

Aki was special. She was smart enough to realize that. Aki had to be strong. She couldn't show any weakness, never again. If she pleaded, they took advantage of her. If she cried, they laughed at her. If she ran, she lost. So, to protect herself, Aki bottled everything in, let nothing out; she strengthened her will . . . and waited.

The emotions she killed made her unflappable. Her loathing for others gave her an acid tongue. Powerful feelings of superiority and inferiority hardened her exterior, and she unconsciously tried to remain calm and collected in every situation.

Aki was brilliant and foolish, strong and weak.

She put up with everything—until she at last advanced to Seisou University High School, miles from home. Finally, she was free.

Aki refused to live in a dorm. Nine years of school had left her with a strong fear and mistrust of society. Well aware of this, her parents had agreed. That's why she lived in an apartment, alone.

Ultimately, though, her fears had been proven ungrounded. Nobody here knew the label she'd been given in elementary school. Seisou was a college prep school, with students from all around the country, so Aki was treated as a slightly unusual but otherwise normal student.

Aki projected warped calm, unflappable intelligence, and strength. The people around her took this at face value. And for the first time, she was accepted. It was a whole new world to her.

And it was at Seisou that Aki met someone who smelled the same as she did: Kyoichi Utsume.

A few days after meeting him, she realized he had the same thing lurking in his background as she did. Observation powers heightened through experience told her that Utsume was the same as her. They way he avoided unnecessary contact with other people was a good sign he'd been persecuted, too.

At first, she felt repelled. Soon, this feeling was replaced by shock at his abilities. When she realized how much they transcended her own, she also realized that she couldn't take her eyes off him. It was the first time she'd ever felt love this clearly.

She never wavered.

Yet she gently sealed off her feelings, hiding them inside her calm. Displaying her feelings would lead to shame; experience had taught her that. Anger, sadness, happiness—letting people know how she felt would lead only to snickering.

Aki had no way of dealing with her emotions except trapping them beneath logic. Even when it came to love, she had only one choice: Wait it out.

She was waiting still.

She effortlessly hid her feelings for Utsume. Cold, collected, analytical, and sharp tongued—this was her identity. Now, however, there was a little fretting whirlpool inside her that she couldn't identify. She could feel panic building without knowing the reason—or where it would lead.

Was she worried because Utsume was in danger? Or was it that she wanted to kill Ayame?

"We have to help Kyo," Aki said, stamping down her emotions.

First, the hospital.

No more thoughts. They weren't leading anywhere.
She could think about it later.

Three

They took the bus to town. The hospital was a twenty-minute walk from there.

Aki and Ryoko stood outside, looking up at it.

"Well, it certainly is intimidating."

"I hear about it all the time, but I've never seen it up close before."

The white building gleamed against the dark sky.

The Naijin Association Foundation Hospital was outside the city, with almost no homes built near it. Framed by the forest behind it, the building looked like a big, long, white box, surrounded and protected by a wall ten feet tall. And that was when it was seen from a distance; now that they were this close, the wall was the only thing they could see. It was daunting, to say the least.

So much so, it was hard to believe the sturdy wall's defenses were aimed not at those outside, but at those inside.

"Naijin Association Foundation Hospital—Psychiatry, Neurology, etc." said the simple, unadorned plate on the wall. There was an intercom next to the front gate, and Aki pushed the button. It made no noise. It must have worked, though, because a few seconds later, a voice came back.

"Yes?"

"Uh, um . . . I'm seeking admittance," Aki said, stammering.

The voice sounded like it belonged to an elderly man. "Do you have a referral slip?"

"Um, yes."

"What's the number?"

"Hang on . . . 00154297."

"Let me check that. Please wait."

And the intercom shut off, making no further sound. It was a curt, businesslike reception.

"I guess they don't need our names?" Ryoko asked, anxious.

Aki shrugged, disinterested.

Finally, the intercom crackled back to life. "Sorry about that. Everything checked out. Is number 00154296 with you, as well?"

"Huh?"

"Oh, you mean me?" Ryoko said, pulling out her own referral slip.

"Oh, right," Aki said. "She's with me."

"Okay. See the little door on the right? The automatic lock will open for one minute only, so enter quickly. Then, wait at the front entrance to the building. Someone will come to meet you there. Please, don't wander around."

The intercom switched off. Instantly, there was a series of ominous clanks as several locks thumped open.

"Yikes!" Ryoko said, alarmed.

Aki never wavered. She made a beeline for the door, calling over her shoulder, "Come on!"

Ryoko didn't move. She was petrified.

"It's unlocked only for a minute!" Aki said, opening the thick door with several locks along the edge. The springs were very strong, so it took an effort to hold it open.

"Come on!" Aki said as she stepped inside.

The path from the gate to the front entrance was eerily silent. Aki ignored this and moved forward.

"Ah! Wait, Aki!" Ryoko said, chasing after her.

When they both were inside, the door swung shut and the locks thumped closed again. There was no other sound. Silence settled on the hospital again, as if it always had been there.

"We heard about you from Shuzenji. My name is Kijou, and I'll be in charge of this matter," said the black-clothed man who came out to meet them.

Aki and Ryoko gaped.

The man wore a suit. In all other respects, however, he was clearly the same man they'd met at Shuzenji.

Neither girl knew how to react.

"What is it?" Kijou said, puzzled.

Even his body language was the same as the priest's.

"How did you get ahead of us?" Aki asked. "Is this some sort of joke?"

Kijou grasped her meaning at once, hurriedly explaining, "Oh, no! We're twins. You met my brother, Atsushi. My name is Yutaka."

"Twins?"

He handed her his card. It was a simple business card: "Kijou Yutaka, Civil Servant, Tel 090-****-**** (c)."

"Civil servant?" Aki asked, suspicious.

"Basically, yes," Kijou said calmly. "It's neither a lie, nor the full truth, but somewhere in between. To be more accurate, I'm a secret agent."

"Huh?" Aki said skeptically. The priest had said there was an expert on these matters in the hospital. Aki had assumed that he'd be a doctor of some kind. "You aren't a psychiatrist?"

"No," Kijou said, shaking his head. "I've been trained in psychology and counseling as a prerequisite, and I have been known to call myself a doctor if the situation calls for it. In this case, however, I don't see the need."

"I'm not sure what you mean," Aki said, glancing at the man's hands. "Do you also occasionally call yourself a priest?"

"Of course," he said, without hesitating.

Aki frowned. Was he making fun of them? His language and bearing were different, but a little acting would take care of that. The more she thought about it, the more he seemed to resemble the priest with his counselor-like behavior.

Were they really twins? Were they the same person?

Aki stared at the man's Rolex.

"I can't help but think you're treating us like we're idiots," she said.

Kijou replied, "I don't mind. After all, we aren't here to discuss my identity." This effectively ended the conversation, and he led them into the hospital.

As they walked down the brightly lit white hallway, Kijou began, "Considering both of you have seen one of them, I'm sure you will agree that your situation is not one that a little counseling can clear up."

"Yeah," Aki agreed.

"It isn't a hallucination, it isn't your imagination, and it isn't the result of any mental problem. They actually exist, and any number of people have fallen prey to them over the years. They have been with us for a very, very long time. If we don't do something, then your Utsume will be consumed by them, and he will die."

That didn't sound good.

"They have existed for a long time, and mankind has fought them, things like them, or their relatives, throughout all that time. As time goes on, the people, the tools, and the means of fighting have changed, but the pattern remains the same. Mankind always has been on the defensive. It was easier once. Death and disappearances were a part of daily life. That is no longer the case."

"Death isn't part of daily life? People still die, don't they?"

"Not the same way. We have built systems to deal with it, governments to keep records on every one of us. Once, when people vanished, it was like they never existed. Now, a report will be filed. If they are killed, the police will investigate, and it will be on the news. And what would happen if people knew a death had been caused by something inhuman? Pandemonium!"

"Right."

"Unnatural events also are not as widely accepted as they once were. That's not at all a bad thing. With just this one exception, science is king. Don't worry about that." He sighed. "As long as that one exception exists, the world needs people like us . . . until science has managed to explain the exception."

Kijou opened a door marked "Reception Room No. 7."

"Welcome to the Agency. Allow me to prove that the scientific method works on all things. After all, our organization exists to fight beings like them."

He grinned, waving them inside.

Aki said nothing. The plate of poison she'd begun digesting at Shuzenji had turned out to be piled higher than she'd guessed.

"Whatever happens, happens," Aki thought. Without further ado, she stepped into the reception room.

Four

There was nothing in the room but a sofa, a desk, and a chair.

The two girls sat opposite Kijou.

"Are you comfortable?" he asked.

Then, he began, "The scientific method is not about running all phenomenon through a filter of scientific knowledge so that we can deny everything that doesn't fit. It's about believing that all results have a cause—and attempting to discover what that cause is."

"Really?" Ryoko said, astonished.

Aki growled, "You're supposed to know that."

"It's true. It's possible to discover the cause for anything. No matter how absurd or impossible or incoherent something may appear to be, there always is a cause. By investigating, pondering, and building on what we have learned, we seek to fight what the world believes to be supernatural phenomenon."

Kijou handed them each a bundle of paper, taken from the desktop.

"What's this?"

"This is one of our weapons, the Delta Paranormal Susceptibility Test. I'm going to have you both take this index now. It will measure the strength of what often is called the 'sixth sense.'"

"Huh," Aki said, flipping through the packet of extremely nice paper.

The pages were printed with not only words but also colorful illustrations and patterns. Down one side of the page was an answer sheet, a grid of circles designed to be machine-read. Aki had never seen an answer sheet built into a test booklet before.

"That's weird," she said.

"We do it that way to remove the time lag between thinking and marking your answer. All the questions are 'yes or no' responses, but you're allowed only five seconds to read and answer each one. There's an alarm every five seconds and vocal instructions on these," he said, handing over a thin pair of headphones to each girl. He also placed two trays with ten sharpened pencils each in front of them. He certainly was prepared.

"So . . ." Kijou said, looking pressed for time.

They filled in the dots on the first page for their age and gender. Both put on the headphones.

"Ready?"

Aki and Ryoko nodded.

"There are three-hundred eighty problems in all. Please begin."

Kijou pushed a switch, and a woman's voice began counting down. "Three. Two. One. Start."

The girls opened the test booklets and began.

The test was a trifle odd, but it basically was the same as any personality test.

Aki tried to make a conscious effort to analyze the test as she went, but the vocal instructions coming over the headphones were relentless and banished all other thoughts: "Problem one. Five seconds. Three. Two. One. Finished. Please mark your answer. Problem two. Five seconds. . . ."

1. Death is frightening.   Yes/No

2. I like animals.   Yes/No

3. I hate my mother.   Yes/No

4. I hate my father.   Yes/No

5. I believe in ghosts.   Yes/No

6. I have faith in something.   Yes/No

7. I often feel sympathy for the dead.   Yes/No

8. People often tell me I daydream a lot.   Yes/No

At first, the test concentrated on personality and thoughts, asking about family, experiences, and knowledge. Every now and then, there would be an extremely strange question, but there was no time to think about that.

The sentences seemed to be getting gradually longer. If this was intended to steadily increase the pressure by intervals, then the test had been well designed.

52. Some member of my immediate family, my grandparents, or my great-grandparents often told me fairytales.   Yes/No

53. I have received counseling, treatment, or medication for a mental condition with subjective symptoms.   Yes/No

On the questions went.

Aki and Ryoko slowly were led into a state of intense focus, answering question after question.

They no longer had any time to wonder at the direction of the questions.

And just as they had fallen into this state, just as they no longer were able to think about anything except the next answer, the nature of the questions shifted dramatically.

159. I know "that" hand [Audio voice: "YYHERRRRRLYHP"]
can reach the moon.   Yes/No

All along, there had been occasional questions that seemed meaningless or disjointed, but now the number of these began to increase. There were impossible-to-read words, rows of letters, and phrases that couldn't be taken as questions.

The grammar began to splinter, becoming too poetic or too philosophical to understand. Rows of unidentifiable symbols were printed tightly together.

And yet, the test still demanded a selection: either yes or no.

Soon, there were no sentences at all. There would be a figure that looked like something from a history textbook, followed, without explanation, by "Yes/No," or a garishly colored abstract painting, followed by "Yes/No."

They were forced to answer "yes" or "no" to an ordinary landscape photograph, a color bar from a sample book, a picture of some kind of beetle.

There was a pointillism picture done with what looked like particles of light; an array of tarot cards; a selection of complicated, vivid patterns; even a shifting hologram.

Next came a detailed still life, like an instruction manual; then, a photograph enlarged so much it was impossible to make out; now, a sketch of some uncanny living thing, followed by a complicated, difficult labyrinth.

Every picture or pattern demanded an answer: yes or no.

They had no time to wonder at the unnatural content. They had no time to wonder which was "yes" and which was "no." They had long since fallen into a sort of hypnotic trance, mechanically answering "yes" or "no" as their feelings led them.

Propelled onward by the rhythm of the voice in their ears, they fell naturally into that state, their eyes automatically roaming over each question.

So, when Kijou said, "That's it! You're done," Aki felt as if she'd just woken up. The feeling reminded her of having finished taking an exam or reading the last page of a really gripping novel. There was that same fatigued stiffness in her shoulders.

Ryoko groaned and stretched.

Kijou handed their test sheets to somebody through the door before resuming his seat. "Now, there are a few things I need to explain before your results come back," he said, leaning back in his chair.

"Then, let me ask," Aki said. "What was that test?"

"It's strange, isn't it?"

Aki clearly thought that was an understatement.

Kijou laughed.

"It's designed to lead you into a hypnotic state. A psychologist by the name of John Delta invented it. With that test alone, we can determine the power of your sixth sense with a seventy-two percent certainty; and with an additional background worksheet, we can get that up to eighty-four percent. Current beliefs categorize sixth sense as a psychological characteristic, you see. Doctor Delta is dead, though, so we have no idea how, exactly, the Delta test measures the sixth sense."

"You don't know how it works, but you're using it anyway?" Aki asked scornfully.

"Yes," Kijou said, as if Aki had a good point. "We do know that it's effective, though. The test was found among the doctor's things when he died. To begin with, nobody knew what it was supposed to test, so it was ignored for a long time—especially considering the doctor also was an occultist, which put him at the fringes of his profession."

This was too suspicious to warrant a comment.

"However, we use what we can. We need this test. We can't afford to bring people who are easily entranced by beings from another world on the scene when we go hunting."

"What?" Kijou said the word so casually that Aki almost missed it. "You *hunt* them?"

"Of course. We can't kill them, but we can chase them away. We're a kind of quarantine agency, and we've been amassing techniques to deal with them for a long time. We battle the harm these beings cause, preventing it from spreading. When people meet with supernatural events, they may not be able to understand the cause and might be afraid; even if you don't know the cause, though, there are ways to resist. Before we discovered microorganisms, we were using disinfectant; it's the same idea. We continue to study them as we fight; someday, we finally may understand what these paranormal phenomenon are, and then we finally may know how to kill them."

Aki was unable to let herself be impressed. If they actually could save Utsume, however, then she considered his explanation very good news.

"Tell me about her," Aki said.

Kijou nodded. Then, he stared at the ceiling, as if trying to figure out where to begin.

"First of all, we tend to refer to supernatural phenomena as if they were a type of virus," he explained. "Why do we do this? Well, these beings do not just attack any old human. They aren't lying in wait. Like germs, they are transmitted from one person to another."

"Huh?" Aki frowned, not expecting any of this. "What do you mean?"

"Right, I should start at the beginning. People with a sixth sense—what we call 'people susceptible to the paranormal'—are about seventy to eighty percent of the population, on average."

"That many?"

"Yes. Mind you, that 'on average' part is pretty important. The sixth sense is rarely permanent. In extreme cases, it might be here today and gone tomorrow, or it might appear suddenly, without any previous sign of it during a person's life.

"There are two basic types of sensitives: latent sensitives and active sensitives. Actually, there is a third type—the absolute sensitive—but this is exceptionally rare, less than one percent, so we can omit it. The ratio of latents to actives is about eighty to twenty."

"And what we usually refer to as psychic people are this active type?" Aki asked.

"Yes, exactly," Kijou replied, nodding vigorously. It was impossible to tell if he was sincere.

"People with unrealized potential are latents; I understand that much. But how are ghosts transmitted through humans? You can't mean that once a ghost has possessed someone, it can be passed along by touch or become airborne?" Aki's voice had deepened. She sounded gruff, like an elementary school bully.

Kijou chuckled, shaking his head. "Of course not. The fundamental principle there is wrong. These beings do not come from the outside, take possession of a human, and cause harm. They come from inside the human heart."

Ryoko raised her hand. "Teacher, that last bit went over my head."

Aki agreed. "It sounds like you're telling us to go to the shrink because we're seeing things," she said snidely.

"Oh no, I didn't," Kijou said weakly. "When I say they come from inside the human heart, I mean it in the occult sense rather than the psychological sense. Have you heard the theory that people's hearts all are connected in the subconscious, at the base of the id?"

"Eh?" Ryoko frowned.

Aki had read about this somewhere. "It's often compared to the ripples from a large wave, right? Each crest of the waves is an individual's conscious mind; if you go down the wave, the unconscious mind spreads out. Then, at the very bottom, well below the ego, they all are connected."

She thought she'd read that in a book about Jungian psychology. In a book she'd read more recently, though, the lower portions were not connected; instead, they were described as being like half spheres.

Kijou nodded. "That's correct. Our current theory says that these beings are from the collective unconscious. None of us are able to perceive our subconscious, so these beings are outside the realm of human knowledge. But everyone's mind is connected fundamentally to the other world. If the right conditions are met, things no human can comprehend will come rising out of the depths and into the conscious mind," he said gravely.

If this were true, it was very frightening. Aki groaned. It was a groan of doubt. "That's a little—"

"Well, the chances are extremely remote. If you lead a normal life, nothing like that ever will happen. Several conditions have to be met before it can."

Suddenly, Aki got it. "Do you mean that the 'infectious' part is those conditions?"

Kijou whistled. "Exactly! You are a smart one. I'm very impressed," he said, clapping.

Aki glared at him. "Flattery will get you nowhere."

"Harsh," Kijou said, unmoved. He continued as if nothing at all had happened, "So, what exactly is it that gets transmitted? I described it as a virus earlier, but it operates more like a computer virus."

"A computer virus?"

"Yes. In order for these beings to harm anyone, two conditions must be met. First, the hardware must be capable of receiving them—in other words, the person must be susceptible to the paranormal, must have an active sixth sense. Second, they have to install the software—a program that guides them to our consciousness."

"Huh."

"If we imagine the collective unconscious—the other world—as if it were the Internet, then all of our minds are computers connected on a network.

"For the majority, the program that allows the network connection is not operating, or it never was installed in the first place. There are some people with absolutely no sixth sense, who fall in the latter category. Most people are capable of having a sixth sense; however, it just hasn't manifested yet.

"On the other hand, once these connections are working, people can access the 'net—or the collective unconscious—whenever they want. These people are psychics. Still, a computer can't connect to the Internet with only the hardware."

"You also need a Web browser or an e-mail program."

"Right. That is what infects. When we get the software from other people, we can touch the other world."

Aki frowned. "I'm not sure I follow."

"Fair enough. Frankly, these beings are so fundamentally different from humans that we are unable to imagine them—as long as we lead normal lives and don't reach down into the depths of our subconscious. Once a chance is given, however, people become capable of looking into those depths."

"Like, people suddenly realize why they have a certain habit if someone points it out to them?"

"Basically. This also is true for the other world. If there are no roads, they're unable to travel up into our subconscious."

"For crying out loud!" Aki snapped, growing frustrated with Kijou's roundabout explanation. "Get to the point! What, exactly, is it, this 'software'?"

Kijou sighed. He slightly lowered his voice before saying, "Basically? Ghost stories. Makes sense, doesn't it? Knowledge about unnatural things is the key to bringing them into your consciousness. We always are in contact with that other world. If we don't know that, it's the same as if we aren't. The moment we know about the other world, though, we become capable of seeing it, and *they* will try to assimilate us. You could say that our world already is being invaded by theirs—and the moment people find out about it, it turns its claws on them."

Neither Aki nor Ryoko said anything. There was a long silence.

Chapter 5:

Daily Life

One

"Call if anything happens."

Yesterday—no, to be strictly accurate, early this morning, Kijou had put the two girls in a taxi, cautioning them not to tell anyone about the Agency.

He had taken only a short nap since then. There were no windows in the Naijin Association Foundation Hospital, so time was nothing more than numbers.

The documents he had requested from the information bureau steadily poured in: everything from rumors collected in the area to information on the people believed connected to this case (or their relatives or families). Among the documents were copies of the girls' report cards and their medical histories. The Agency didn't fuss about invasion of privacy. If they felt it was important, they would go so far as to acquire pediatric records on how the girls' bodies had developed in elementary school.

If that strong-willed girl, Kidono, could see all this, how would she react? Kijou imagined she had no idea her mother's family, until three generations ago, had been linked to inugami, the dog gods.

Kijou shook his head at this uncharacteristic thought. Maybe he really was tired.

He knew full well that they needed this information. Take the hospital records, for example. If there were any history of mental illness, then the chances of that person being susceptible to the paranormal increased dramatically.

The report cards told them about students' personalities and behavior, and occasionally any trouble or accidents they'd been involved with, making them a key piece of information about the students' background. It wasn't much, but occasionally it could provide important insights into intellectual abilities.

If there had been any, the police would've provided records regarding the girls, too.

And, if necessary, the Agency would collect newspaper articles or dispatch an investigator to the girls' family homes. For instance, Aki was connected to a tsukimono-suji; depending on the result of her Delta Paranormal Susceptibility Test, she might be marked down as someone to watch in the future.

Fortunately, both girls had tested positive as latents.

It was vitally important that cases like this, relating to beings like these, be viewed objectively. If he overlooked anything, it could lead to tragedy. He had to think of every possibility, eliminate every danger. There was no room for emotion.

Kijou picked up two fax pages from one of the Agency's information pools: his brother who worked at Shuzenji.

"Unbelievable," he said. When these had first arrived and he'd heard a pair of high school girls had provided them, Kijou had been genuinely terrified.

They were copies from a book about regional legends and a study of urban legends. Each of them seemed perfectly ordinary, but the combination was very bad, indeed. There were some "stories" in this world that really were nonfiction, and they were forbidden—because just knowing the story could summon *them*. This *Modern Urban Legends* was one such book, and the Agency had worked hard to remove all copies from circulation.

In all likelihood, that book had caused all of this to happen. The other book, the book of old stories, probably was reality-based, as well. The kami-kakushi featured in these books was almost certainly the enemy this time. It was rare for these stories to spread through books; but when they did, it was on an explosive scale, a force to be reckoned with.

Modern Urban Legends was a small-press book aimed at enthusiasts. Most copies were in private libraries, so the Agency had been unable to collect them all.

Oosako Eiichiro had published an awfully high percentage of stories that were real; so it came as no surprise when Kouji heard the author recently had been placed under observation by the Agency.

The studies he wrote contained more than two genuine cases per volume, which was an extraordinarily high success rate. If he was doing it unconsciously, it was nothing short of miraculous . . . so, there was a good chance that he was well aware of what he was doing.

There were several books in front of Kijou. All of them had been provided by the information bureau and were considered top secret. In other words, all of them were books that shouldn't be read by someone who hadn't received counseling and hypnotic treatment to deactivate susceptibility to the paranormal. If they were found in public, they were to be collected at once and treated as highly dangerous materials.

"And stories of this type are found all over the world. In Europe, there are stories of the fairies stealing human children (and even a few where humans steal fairy children). If we combine those stories with legends of an invisible fairy city—circles where fairies can dance, but if humans enter, they will vanish—then stories of kami-kakushi increase dramatically in number, creating an entire genre in their own right. This suggests that unnatural beings that

cause disappearances actually do exist all over the world." — Oosaka Eiichiro, *On Kami-kakushi*

"*These ancient stories may spread in many different places following the exact same motifs. For instance, the belief that a dramatic event can break a curse is seen in our Japanese* Tanishi Musuko, *as well as the Grimm Brother's* Frog Prince. Yonefuku-Awafuku *is similar to* Cinderella. *There are stories all over the world about buying and selling dreams, and the concept of bones that tell how they were killed also is common. Sometimes, we can prove these stories were passed across Asia; but it is more entertaining to take a flight of fancy, like your author, and believe them to be proof that incidents like these actually happened—and beings like these are, in fact, scattered all across the world."* — Oosaka Eiichiro, *Folklore and Children's Tales*

"*We might call them 'urban legends,' but some of the many stories collected here clearly follow the same motifs as the old stories from folklore. Urban legends tend to demand a certain level of reality and avoid obvious lies, so this phenomenon is extremely curious. It proves these old motifs, despite their years of use, still possess a certain kind of reality, even in a modern setting. As if they actually have existed since ancient times. For example, motif 12115 (see page 213) is found in the modern stories of the kami-kakushi."* — Oosaka Eiichiro, *Modern Urban Legends*

This stuff was terrifying. The Agency carefully classified all accurate information on the other world. Kijou had no idea how the man had reached these conclusions—or delusions—but for an independent researcher to get this far was astonishing. *He had not made a single mistake.*

Possibly, his writings were nothing more than idle flights of fancy. The author might be prone to hallucinations, which had given rise to deranged conclusions—but it wasn't the author's intentions that mattered; it was the people who read his work and thought, "That makes sense." The author might not believe a word of it; if his readers did, however, then there was a chance that the real truth would spread explosively. This was the Agency's greatest fear.

Average citizens were both smarter and more foolish than they themselves realized. It was not an overreaction for the Agency to watch the media and the publishing houses, applying pressure when needed.

Sometimes, people simply would figure out things. The Agency always was on the lookout for the information those types were spreading. Whether operatives like Kijou were active or on standby, the information bureau ceaselessly sifted through information, looking for anything dangerous. Even now, somewhere in Japan, black-suited agents were approaching people who *knew,* warning them not to tell anyone.

They had only one goal: stopping these beings from spreading.

To cut off a source of dangerous rumors, the men in black would monitor their targets, approach them, destroy all evidence, and order them to forget all about it.

If the target refused, they would take the person away and erase their memories. There were more complicated means of information control, as well, if the situation called for them.

Eventually, these girls would have their memories erased.

Surveillance, intimidation, and disposal—all these methods were to protect the world's tranquility. Society was able to succeed only because of these secret missions.

Kijou knew this was true. Still, he felt a touch of sadness.

"What's wrong with me?" he muttered with a self-deprecating grin.

Certainly, those girls had been engaging: clever, compassionate, and collected. He had cut off all contact with her when he had entered the Agency, but his own daughter must be about their age now; she would be attending a private high school, as well. Circumstances prevented him from meeting her, but he was pleased by the idea that she had been brought up as splendidly as these girls he'd just met.

But . . . but *what?* He hadn't forgotten his duty. Intelligence did not grant them any special rights. He had explained about the other world only to temporarily satisfy them, to keep them from telling anyone else. He had given them the bare minimum of information needed to achieve that result. Eventually, when the situation had been dealt with properly, those memories would be wiped clean. This was inevitable, unquestionable.

He had given them no more information than they needed. For instance, he did not share that ever since Seisou High School's construction, there had been stories about a girl's ghost, whose description perfectly matched Ayame's. The girls, after all, had not heard the stories.

And he did not share that the focal point of this incident, Kyoichi Utsume, had been involved in a remarkably similar case ten years before; ever since, his movements had been monitored closely by the information bureau.

He hadn't told the girls either of these things because they didn't need to know.

The Agency was so named precisely because of the requisite level of secretiveness. Just as the nondescript name suggested—no, more than it suggested, the Agency dealt in things best kept under wraps, things no one else could know—starting with the very existence of these beings.

Furthermore, operatives like Kijou, commonly referred to as "hunter agents," were all listed as deceased; for all intents and purposes, they did not exist.

Of course, Kijou had not told the girls this, either; it was all considered classified.

There was no problem. He had made no mistakes. All he had to do was follow the standard mission pattern: Search and destroy. After the information bureau found the target, he would take care of disposal, as he always did.

Nothing was wrong. It's true that he had allowed himself to feel sympathetic. But there was nothing out of the ordinary, no problem at all.

Two

Takemi Kondou was in his first period class.

"Ugh." His expression slackened—for the simple reason that his brain seemed to be doing the same. There was no way he could remember English this early in the morning, he thought, resting his chin on his hand—especially on a Saturday. A few hours from now, he would be free, the knowledge of which was making it impossible for him to concentrate and work diligently.

The teacher's voice seemed so far away. Or perhaps, his own mind had drifted off somewhere.

Takemi desperately thought about anything besides class, struggling to keep awake. He hadn't gotten enough sleep: Too much had happened yesterday, and he'd tossed and turned all night.

Although he'd been through the same thing, Toshiya was sitting there as if nothing had happened, which Takemi found unacceptable. Bitterly jealous, Takemi pondered that Toshiya's nerves must be made of something much thicker than his own—like high-voltage cable in comparison to thin electrical wire.

That man, Jinno Kageyuki . . . Takemi shuddered. Meeting a self-described psychic and talking with him . . . after an experience like that, how could anyone return to life like ordinary? Takemi refused to believe it was possible.

None of it made any sense.

Yesterday, after Jinno had vanished into thin air, as a magician might be expected to, Takemi and Toshiya had left the shop to find the full moon shining in the clear sky above.

The clock said nine. They'd entered the shop around six, so they had been there for three hours. Takemi could've sworn they'd been in there no more than an hour, though.

He now understood the fairytale about the fisherman and the turtle—and how Urashima Tarou must have felt. There was no mistake about it, and only people who hadn't met Jinno could say there was. That man was not natural.

"So weird!" Takemi moaned.

He'd considered going back to that shop to make sure; but the more he thought about it, the less he wanted to do it. Although Takemi was scared of Jinno, he found something else more frightening: He probably wouldn't be able to find the shop again. If that happened, Takemi would become even more terrified.

For the life of him, he couldn't remember the shop's name, nor could he find the box of matches with the map on the back. Takemi accepted that it simply was that kind of place, and he'd given up resisting.

When everyone had met in the morning, Takemi had not wanted to say anything. Toshiya obviously had no intention of explaining anything. Takemi thought it was a little unfair, but he ultimately said nothing either. He couldn't believe what he had seen—how could he tell someone else about it?

Oddly, neither Aki nor Ryoko asked.

They had said 'hello,' but otherwise they seemed to have nothing much to say.

"Good morning."

"Mm, morning."

"Any luck yesterday?"

"Hm, not much. You?"

"Um, yeah, nothing worth mentioning."

"Oh."

That had been the extent of it.

Although Takemi found their reticence a bit odd, he just assumed they hadn't discovered anything and were a little embarrassed about it. Or perhaps, something had happened to them . . . ? Fear that pressing the issue would backfire led him to decide to let sleeping dogs lie.

Neither group had found out anything, really—at least, nothing they would admit to.

Takemi wanted a little more time to think.

A dry tapping filled the room: the noise of chalk slowly grinding away on the blackboard. The sound was hypnotic, inviting him to sleep. The teacher seemed to be writing English syntax on the board. Apparently, if you wrote something boring, the noise it made was equally dull.

Without thinking at all, Takemi copied down the board's contents into his notebook. He paid no attention; after all, everyone knew that, come test time, learning this stuff was not nearly as useful as memorizing a single page from the vocabulary book.

So, Takemi could think things through as much as he liked.

Utsume was still missing. Naturally, he hadn't called. The school didn't make occasional absences an issue. If you missed two or three days, though, they'd call your home. Obviously, even that action had failed to change anything.

Takemi couldn't imagine where Utsume might be, or what he might be doing. If the world Utsume was lost in was the same one that Takemi had experienced two nights ago, though, then it was a horrible place to be.

Jinno had told them what could happen to the kami-kakushi's victims. Every possibility boiled down to Utsume's death. As Toshiya had listened, his expression had betrayed his desire to throw himself at Jinno; after all, the magician's predictions all amounted to nothing more than prophecies of doom for Utsume. Who could blame Toshiya for becoming upset?

Still . . . it just didn't seem real to Takemi. Utsume wasn't the kind of person who got himself into trouble. He was too much in control: No matter what happened, he never panicked. Takemi couldn't picture him in danger, struggling to get out. He was groundlessly optimistic on this point. After all, if Utsume had been taken to another world, he hardly would give up. He would think things through calmly and take action.

What would His Majesty do? Takemi thought. *What did the Dark Prince go to that other world to do?* If he'd allowed himself to be captured, then he must've had a goal. *How does His Majesty plan to escape the other world?* If he had been captured against his will, then Utsume would think of a way out. *How can I help the Prince of Darkness?* If Utsume was trying to escape from the other world on his own, then there might be something they could do from this side, Takemi thought. *What is His Majesty trying to do?*

His thoughts ground to a halt. *It's impossible for an idiot like me to pull off a high-level stunt like tracing the Dark Prince's thoughts.* . . . He despaired at his own limitations, staring at the ceiling. Takemi had said something like this aloud once before, he remembered.

"Kondou. Never settle for suspension of thought." That had been Utsume's somewhat scornful response. "You can call yourself an idiot as much as you like. You can believe it, even. But don't use that as a reason to stop thinking. That's where genuine stupidity begins."

At the time, Takemi habitually called himself an idiot. It was this one day that Utsume happened to hear it.

"Listen, Kondou. People who think they are intelligent actually tend to be smarter than average. This is because once they believe this to be true, they begin to act like it is. They are imposing their own thoughts on themselves. Every time they think, they are striving for the intelligence they so desire. In other words, more than anyone else, they are trying to think.

"You see? That's the key. The brain is sharpened by use. If you force yourself to think, then your mind will continue to improve. No matter how stupid people look, if they enjoy thinking, then their brains are developed somewhere. As long as they correctly grasp the direction of their own abilities, they will have great power.

"So, Kondou, never stop thinking. It's easy to stop; but if you settle for it, it will damage the development of your mind. Logic, calculations, imagination—think anything at all. But think. Use your mind, make it better. If you think, your brain will respond. That's what your brain is for."

"Some minds are still better than others."

"Who cares? You can't tell how good a brain is from the outside. Nobody in the world knows his own talents. If nobody knows, then we're all starting from the same place.

"Learn by using, like you would any tool—that's the only way to discover your own abilities."

So said the Dark Prince of the Literature Club, Kyoichi Utsume. It all seemed a little absurd to Takemi now; at the time, however, he'd been overwhelmed by Utsume's charisma. He had stopped calling himself an idiot. Almost.

"Think," Takemi whispered.

Judging from his experience so far, Utsume almost never did anything without a reason. And he definitely never did anything without thinking. Regardless of the cause, Utsume hated to do anything meaningless. He attempted to control everything that involved him.

Which means . . . ? Takemi frowned.

Utsume's personality meant it was impossible for him do something without meaning. Which meant that everything Utsume did before he disappeared must have had some significance. So, if Takemi were to analyze Utsume's actions, then . . . *I'd know exactly what His Majesty was doing!* Takemi was excited by his own idea, hardly believing his own mind had produced such a beautiful notion. *If I took them apart, all Utsume's actions would make sense.* This was amazing. Takemi felt a mystery-novel level of catharsis.

He searched his memory for everything Utsume had done. Then, once he had listed everything, he started to analyze . . . and failed. He had hit on something inexplicable and gotten stuck: *Why did the Dark Prince introduce everyone to his girlfriend?* Takemi had no idea. *What did that mean?*

His deductions never got past that. Takemi's thoughts stayed immobile for the rest of class.

Three

"For you, not a bad idea. Everything after that is a mess, though." Aki was the first to respond.

"Sorry," Takemi said, sulking.

Saturday classes had ended. By noon, school had finished for the day. All through second and third period, Takemi had failed to reach any conclusions. So, he had gathered everyone together in a corner of the empty classroom and told them his idea, hoping they could help. No sooner had he finished than Aki had unleashed her tongue at him.

"I'm right, though, aren't I?" he said, defensively.

"Yeah, it's a decent observation," Aki admitted, giving it some thought.

Takemi beamed. This was probably the most praise he would ever receive from her. Although he knew better, he couldn't help but feel proud . . .

. . . until Aki added, "You should've been able to construct at least one theory, though."

"Ack." Takemi flinched in pain. It was true. He couldn't argue. Instead, Takemi deflated. He dramatically clutched his chest and collapsed into a chair.

"Um . . . I think it's amazing, Takemi," Ryoko said in a placating manner. "I wouldn't have thought of it."

"You really think so?"

"Yeah."

"Only Ryoko understands me!"

"Good boy," she said, patting him on the head.

"Ignoring the idiot bonding," Aki said, turning toward Toshiya. "What do you think, Murakami?"

"Makes sense," he said, leaning against the wall, arms folded. "I agree. If Utsume does something unnatural, there must be a reason for it."

"Yeah, I agree with that much of Kondou's idea," Aki nodded. "The strangest part is why he would introduce his girlfriend to us—not only us, Kyo introduced her to everyone he knew, apparently. All kinds of people have been talking about her, asking 'who was that?' and things like that."

"Not normal behavior, especially for him."

"I think if he really were to start going out with someone, Kyo would hold his tongue. 'Peer approval is irrelevant,' right?"

"Sounds like something he'd say."

They all could picture him saying that.

Takemi said, "Why did His Majesty show her around, then?"

"Because he needed to," Aki said. "What would be the normal reason to introduce your new girlfriend to everyone you know? What do you think, Ryoko?"

"Um, you want them all to get along?"

"Doesn't fit. She's not a student here, meaning there's no need to introduce her unless he's bringing her along."

"She's my girlfriend, so hands off?"

"Nope. Same reason."

"Proud that you're going out and want to show her off?"

"Not with Kyo's personality."

"Then, she's so cute you have to share?"

"Least possible of all," Aki said, crossing her arms. "What do you think, Kondou?"

"Mm? Hm . . ." Takemi hesitated. While he was listening to Aki and Ryoko, he had remembered something else: *Utsume had introduced his girlfriend to everyone. . . .* Takemi remembered Jinno's words: "If you're introduced to her, you can see her."

Utsume had made it so quite a lot of people could see Ayame. He'd made as many people as possible capable of seeing the kami-kakushi.

"Not her . . ." Takemi said slowly.

"What?"

"The Dark Prince wasn't introducing her, specifically—he was introducing the kami-kakushi."

Every face in the room stiffened.

"Uh, it was just a thought—didn't mean much by it," Takemi said hastily, surprised by the reaction.

The tension failed to dissipate.

He thoughtlessly had spoken his mind. He glanced at Toshiya for help, but Toshiya was glaring at him reproachfully. Takemi hung his head.

"Kondou . . ." Aki said. "You've outdone yourself today."

Takemi was not the least bit happy, considering his outburst had been a mistake.

Aki scowled at the floor. "Okay, so he was introducing the concept of the kami-kakushi to everyone. Why would Kyo go around attempting to increase the number of victims?"

Takemi was surprised. He had learned about how kami-kakushi worked by talking to Jinno, but it seemed Aki had a pretty fair idea of it herself.

"If it wasn't to increase the number of victims, then why would he show her around? The only one who actually vanished was Kyo. Everyone else is fine. In the end, he was the one who spent the most time with her, so he obviously was going to be her victim. Why introduce her around, then?"

Aki's thoughts were spinning. Reflecting this, her eyes darted here and there.

Ryoko said anxiously, "Aki . . ."

Ignoring her, Aki whispered, "Why? If he already was ready to be her victim, why introduce her? What was the point?" She was lost in thought, even as she spoke.

At last, her gaze locked onto something. "That's possible! Hm."

"You figured it out?" Takemi asked with urgency.

Aki waved a hand, irritated. "It's pure speculation, nothing certain."

"Fine. Tell us!"

"Really?" Aki sighed. "It's not bad speculation . . . one possibility is that, if anything happened to Kyo, then we all would know she was to blame. He drew our attention to her so that, if possible, we would save him. He might be counting on our help. At the least, we would accuse her. That's one possibility."

"Okay."

"Another possibility: He was trying to widen the range of her influence. She could make people she associates with vanish;

so, by dramatically increasing the number of people she associated with, Kyo might have been trying to delay his own disappearance. Second possibility."

"Okay."

"And the final possibility . . . this one's a little out there: He may have been introducing her as a human in an attempt to dilute her nature as a kami-kakushi. Maybe Kyo actually was trying to turn her from a monster into a human.

"You said Kyo's brother was captured by a kami-kakushi? And you said he was still dressed in mourning for his brother? I know this is a bit of a jump, but it's possible he plans to rescue his brother someday. If he could get his hands on a real kami-kakushi, then he'd have taken the first step toward rescuing his brother from their clutches. Maybe."

The confidence drained out of her voice as she spoke, and the last few words were barely audible.

Then, "No, the last one isn't possible. Kyo clearly didn't intend to vanish. If I'm right, then Kyo plans to make it back under his own power or is waiting for us to help him. There's still hope," she said, wrapping things up.

Ryoko's mouth was hanging open.

Takemi was in awe. The last one might have been a leap, but to think of that many possibilities in such a short time . . . ? Takemi and Aki obviously were not operating with the same kind of brain power.

"It . . . it *is* possible," Toshiya said. "We have no guarantee he isn't planning something like that. And we have more than enough grounds to suspect he is. So, that last theory is probable enough. I mean . . . he had good reason to try something risky. We can't rule out something because it's too dangerous. He let that kami-kakushi get near him knowing full well what it might do. If we still have hope, it's the possibility that Utsume had a back-up plan."

"Right," Aki nodded. "That's a pretty good possibility, though. None of us come anywhere near Kyo in knowledge or intelligence."

"True."

"It makes a big difference when you have Kyo on your side."

Four

That evening, when Takemi got back to the dorm, his roommate Okimoto had not returned yet.

Okimoto was going out with a girl from his club, and he often stayed out with her until curfew. Tonight might be one of those days that Okimoto wouldn't come in through the front door.

Yesterday, Takemi himself had been out late.

Unlike in the girls' dorm, in the boys' dorm, it was easy enough to avoid being caught breaking curfew—as long as your roommate kept quiet. Roommates could be changed once a year, if desired; Takemi and Okimoto had gotten along very well as freshmen, though, so they stayed together—and covered for each other when needed. Neither one ever worried about when the other would get back.

They had made no further progress on Utsume that day. Although they'd seen a glimmer of hope, they'd had to admit they

didn't have any concrete clues. Oddly enough, neither Takemi and Toshiya nor Aki and Ryoko had mentioned anything to the other pair about what they'd done the day before. (Takemi never quite worked up the nerve to talk about Jinno, so this suited him fine.) Of course, this meant he was starting to panic: They didn't have the faintest idea where Utsume was.

Outside, night was approaching. Soon, the room would be dark enough that Takemi would have to turn on a light. But the heat from the sunlight that had poured into the room all day long kept the room unexpectedly warm. Takemi took off his coat and threw it on the bed.

He took a deep breath. Then, a thought struck him, and he rummaged through the pockets of his coat, looking for his cell phone. Ever since Utsume had vanished, Takemi had been dialing the Dark Prince's number every chance he got. His cell phone seemed to be the only way they'd be able to contact him directly.

No matter how many times Takemi tried the number, though, Utsume's phone always was out of range, and the calls never went through. Still, Takemi kept calling, because every now and then, he would get a ring instead of the out-of-range message.

In most cases, the phone would ring once and cut off—but it was clear that Utsume had not turned off his phone. If Takemi kept trying, he might get through, eventually.

Takemi found his phone at last. Something else came out with it, tumbling to the floor and rolling across the carpet.

At first, Takemi had no idea what it was. His eyes followed it. Then, a moment later, he remembered.

"Ah!" he cried.

It was the bell, the bell Jinno had given him. He had shoved it in his coat pocket and forgotten about it.

It was supposed to guide him to Utsume. That's what Jinno had said. Takemi didn't believe him, but Jinno made too strong an impression to ignore completely. When he thought about everything that had happened during their encounter with Jinno, just having the bell in his hand creeped out Takemi. The bell genuinely gave him chills.

It felt much like he imagined it would feel to see a photograph of a ghost. The chill that ran down his spine when he'd seen such photographs on TV was very similar. This tiny little bell made such a strong impact that it was amazing he'd forgotten it until now.

Takemi picked up the bell. It didn't make a sound. Despite being empty inside, it was eerily heavy. It must've been made of a particularly heavy metal. Tossing it in his hand, he definitely could feel the weight. It didn't look like it weighed anything, but it certainly felt like it did.

With the exception of the missing clapper, it looked like any other bell, the same kind they sold at every temple or shrine. There was a beautifully woven string attached to it and a jump ring at the end of that, providing a way to attach it to a wallet or anything else.

The string was black and glossy, made of several smooth woven strands. Despite its beauty, Takemi thought there was something almost sinister about it. When one looked closely at the strings, they had the appearance of human hair. This is probably what unnerved Takemi; after all, the black, moist gleam drew your eye to the string, enhancing the overall pressure and sinister feeling.

Takemi stood pondering for a moment, staring at the strange bell. He had no idea what to do with it. It was an unsettling thing—but if it really would take him to Utsume, then how could he throw it away? If you'd been given something by an exceptionally odd person, then you could expect that it would do something exceptionally odd.

After a few minutes spent in agonizing thought, Takemi decided to attach the bell to his cell phone. If it might provide a clue toward finding Utsume, Takemi was prepared to clutch at any straw.

It bothered him that he basically had snatched the bell away from Toshiya. Toshiya might be the rightful owner of the bell, making it ineffective if Takemi had it. The way things had played out, Takemi had carried the bell with him all this time, yet it had proven largely meaningless as nothing had happened yet. He thought perhaps he should give it back to Toshiya tomorrow.

He knew the entire chain of thought was awfully occult, but his experiences over the last few days naturally had led him to that frame of mind, even if he didn't realize it.

"So," he said, hooking the jump ring onto his phone.

Ch-ring.

He could swear he'd heard the bell ring. Takemi frowned slightly. The sound was awfully distinct for it to be his imagination.

The harsh electronic noise his cell phone emitted a moment later made him forget the ringing, though. He almost dropped his phone at the sudden tone he heard. Then, hurriedly, he looked at the screen. He gasped, frozen in place.

Kyoichi Utsume calling.

This shocked Takemi so much that he almost failed to respond. After a long pause, though, he shook himself into action, answering the phone.

Instantly, the world went black. The moment the phone connected, all light vanished from the room, like the breaker had fallen. Goose bumps sprang forth on Takemi's arms and legs. At first, he thought he was frightened, but the chill running down his spine told him otherwise. Even after the wave of fear retreated, the goose bumps remained. The temperature in the room appeared to have dropped several degrees.

The only light in the darkness came from the screen of his cell phone.

The room was filled with frigid air, and a noise like shifting sand came from the phone.

"H-hello? Dark Prince?" Takemi said, his voice trembling despite himself.

No answer. He could hear someone talking quietly, but the sound was faint and drowned out by the static noise. He couldn't make out a word of it. The talking was like an undulating sound behind the white noise; the more he listened, the less certain he was that there were words to be heard.

"Hello? Hello?"

The voicelike sound did not appear to be responding to him.

Shhhhhh . . .

Whisper, whisper . . .

It was whispering something, like some sort of spell— muttering something.

"Hello? Dark Prince? Hellooo . . ."

Mutter . . .

Suddenly, Takemi noticed something: The only sound coming from the cell phone was the white noise. The voice wasn't coming from the phone, only the sound of the sandstorm.

Mutter, mutter . . .

He still could hear the voice. . . . It wasn't coming from the cell phone.

Mutter, mutter, mutter . . .

It slowly dawned on him: The noise was coming from right behind him.

Mutter, mutter . . .

It was in the room.

Takemi couldn't move. The voice was close enough to him that he could make out the words. He could feel it.

He knew: It was standing right there, right behind him. He could feel it. Someone . . . no, some*thing.*

"*Let's go, let's go, together, together, somewhere fun . . .*" The voice whispered. It was getting closer.

A dry mutter, a murmuring whisper. Takemi could hear no footsteps, yet the sound came closer. He could feel it drawing near.

It was right behind him now. He could sense its gaze boring into his back.

It was looking at him.

It was getting closer.

Something, in the darkness . . .

Takemi couldn't turn around.

Oh no! Oh no! His mind was screaming.

The phone had connected, but it shouldn't have. Because the call connected, *it* was here. He had connected to the other world.

He should have realized faster. Why didn't he figure this out before? The air was so different. He should have known. This felt just like the other night. . . .

"*Let's go. Come with me. Come . . .*"

Takemi's teeth chattered. He was shuddering uncontrollably. As cold as it was, though, he couldn't stop sweating. Nor could he move. His body refused to budge. His instincts refused to, as well—refused to turn around. Something was behind him, something he shouldn't see, something terrifying . . . standing right behind him.

It was close enough to touch. He could hear it breathing. It was right up against his back, almost touching his legs, his back, his shoulders, his head.

It was peering past his ear, looking at him. Its gaze, its breath, they brushed past his ear. It was staring at Takemi. Quietly. Then, it moved: Its hands slowly raised up to the level of his head. There was something in those hands. The hands came closer, reaching for his head.

Oh no! Oh no! Takemi knew. He knew what was in its hands. He knew what it was trying to do.

Oh no! Takemi knew. It had a blindfold, and it was going to put it on Takemi. And then, it would take Takemi away.

It . . . it was . . . a kami-kakushi.

All the hairs on Takemi's body stood up.

The thing behind him was what had taken Utsume. It was what had taken Utsume's brother. Utsume's brother had never been seen again. He had been taken away somewhere, and nobody even knew if he was alive.

And now, one of them was standing behind Takemi, whispering and reaching toward him.

"Go, let's go, let's go, let's go, come, let's go, let's . . ."

Takemi's fear erupted. He shrieked, but the shriek never escaped his mouth. He knew it all would be over if the blindfold were placed, yet he couldn't move.

The hands were above his head now, slowly passing over him. The blindfold was almost on.

It was blindfolding him to prevent him from seeing things that should not be seen, a world that should not be seen. If he saw it, he would go mad; and so, it blindfolded him. Once he was blindfolded, he would be ready.

Takemi saw something out of the corner of his eye—not the thing behind him, but something next to his bed: a spongy white mass, the size of a child.

It slithered like a living thing.

Takemi was sure he'd seen it before. A moment later, he remembered: It was one of them, one of the shapeless things that had surrounded Takemi and Ryoko that night.

He had no idea what it was. It looked like nothing in his world. But the moment he recognized that the things poking out of it were armlike, the details became comprehensible, and he was able to process it.

This time, Takemi *did* scream: *It was human.*

Distorted, deformed, unable to maintain its original shape, yet still alive and wriggling.

For some reason, Takemi knew what it was. The knowledge seemed to pour into his mind: It was a failure, a human that had been taken to the other world and was neither able to return home nor to change. This was what happened to those not fortunate enough to remain human or turn into a kami-kakushi. It had been eaten by the other world, melting away before finally becoming unrecognizably deformed.

It was not a human, not a monster, just ugly and pathetic—a detestable thing that no longer possessed a shape of its own.

It shook itself. The five digits sticking directly out of the blob quivered. A tongueless mouth opened in the wrong location, soon drowning beneath melting flesh.

Then, as if seeking help, the blob reached forward. Stretching out of the horrific flesh, the one arm that had kept its original shape scratched at the air.

Takemi recognized that arm's movement: It was the white hand that had grabbed Ryoko that night. This was the one that had grabbed Ryoko!

A new horror ran down his spine, and he shuddered. This was his fate.

At this rate, both Takemi and Utsume would end up like this thing.

Or . . . or was this thing Utsume?

"Come, let's go . . ."

The blindfold lowered. They were almost ready. When they were ready, they would take him. They would take his hand and lead him away—to the other world.

To the other world . . .

To the other world . . .

To the other world . . .

White cloth broke the darkness before his eyes, sliding across his field of vision.

It took Takemi a few minutes to work out that everything had turned white before his eyes because the lights suddenly had turned on. His eyes had grown used to the dark, and they needed a long time before they could perceive the white as light.

He looked around him. He was in his dorm room. Everything unnatural had vanished. Nothing was out of place; it was his room, like always. He turned around nervously, but there was nothing behind him but the stain-covered wall. He could no longer sense *it*.

The phone connection was lost.

For a moment, he thought it all had been a delusion or a daydream. But when he looked at the call history on his phone, it showed he actually had received a call from Utsume. It had lasted less than two minutes. He felt like it had been a lot longer.

Clearly, he had not imagined it. Relief and tension battled within him.

Then, Takemi understood everything: Takemi had survived because Utsume had hung up. The kami-kakushi had appeared only because the phone connected to the other world. When that connection was lost, the kami-kakushi vanished. If the call had lasted a few seconds longer, Takemi would have been taken away. That would have been his last moment in the real world.

He had been saved. Takemi breathed a sigh of relief.

And the phone rang again.

"Eek!" Now, he *did* drop the phone.

This time, though, it wasn't a call—only a message. He picked up his phone, gingerly, as if it were hot.

A different kind of goose bumps appeared on Takemi's arms. The message was from Utsume: *"school cherry."*

That was it. Not what he'd expected. Now that he thought about it, though, it made sense; it had been only a minute since the call had ended, not enough time to write a long message. A message like this, not even bothering with capital letters, was natural. Utsume must have hung up for some reason and then hurriedly written the message. Perhaps, Utsume had saved Takemi; Utsume had realized that Takemi was in danger, so he hung up quickly, changing his tactic.

Even in those circumstances, Utsume had spelled both words correctly. Many students would have dropped a few letters, assuming the meaning would be understood.

This was the first communication from Utsume since he'd vanished. And it was a clear message: Utsume intended to see them again.

He had to tell everyone. Excited, he dialed quickly. The phone began to ring. He could barely stand the wait.

Chapter 6:

And Thus Spoke All of Them

One

Takemi regretted it instantly.

He never should've told Toshiya about Utsume's message first. He had called Toshiya's house first; and no sooner had the words escaped Takemi's mouth than Toshiya had hung up.

"School? You think he wants us to come to school?"

"I don't know, probably—"

Bzzz.

Takemi redialed, thinking they'd been cut off, but one of Toshiya's parents answered, saying their son had run out the door—which left only one explanation: He was moving solo.

Hurriedly, Takemi telephoned Aki, who instantly lit into him. "Obviously, that's what Murakami's going to do! How could you be so stupid?"

"But—"

"Okay, let me handle it. Don't you do anything else. Stay right where you are, do you understand?"

"But—"

Bzzz.

How rude. She didn't bother to listen. He knew it was his fault. Still, what else could he do now but mope?

"'Don't do anything else'? That's just not fair," he muttered. Takemi looked at the clock, but it was too late for dinner—it was already seven thirty.

The way she'd left things, there was nothing Takemi could do but sit and wait for Aki to call back. He was so close to school—only a fifteen-minute walk—and it was agonizing not being able to do anything.

Takemi flopped over on his bed, waiting impatiently.

You could, if you wanted, say that all this progress had been thanks to him. But did he get any acknowledgment? No.

When Takemi went up against someone superior to himself, he dried up instantly. He knew this about himself. While he'd been talking to Aki, he hadn't noticed how unfair she was being. She'd defeated him: Takemi was helping everyone, but Aki had snubbed him.

Sure, he normally might be useless. Sure, he was not nearly as smart as Aki. Still, Takemi had a right to see this thing through. Utsume had sent the message to him, after all.

Takemi stood. Quietly resolved, he took out his spare pair of shoes from under the bed. The front door was near the guard's booth, so you couldn't sneak out that way—which meant it was impossible to get your shoes. Thus, the guys in the dorm all kept a spare pair in case they had to go out the window. Takemi's room was on the first floor, making a window exit easy—and first floor students let everyone on higher floors go through their rooms whenever asked.

"Going out? You?" Okimoto said, surprised. Okimoto had come in through the window, munching on convenience-store *onigiri*.

Takemi nodded. "Yep."

"Okay," Okimoto grinned.

Takemi went out the window.

Like yesterday, the full moon hung in the sky. And Takemi Kondou's strange night was just beginning.

Ryoko and Aki were in the back seat of a black car, driving through the streets of Hazama. Kijou sat in the driver's seat. All three were staring directly in front of them, tension in their faces.

The moon was out. They had known the moon was lurking behind the clouds, but they hadn't realized the full moon was so big. It was almost frightening, Ryoko thought. But she didn't say so.

Instead, she asked about something unrelated, "Isn't it dangerous to wear sunglasses at night?"

Kijou was wearing sunglasses—black clothes, black glasses.

Neither of the others responded.

Had it been that dumb a question? Ryoko looked at her two companions. Aki was ignoring her pointedly. *I guess it was kinda stupid,* Ryoko thought, hanging her head. Or was it something she shouldn't have asked?

"Requirement of the job," Kijou said at last, sounding friendly.

Ryoko shook her head. "Didn't mean it that . . . they look good."

He grimaced. "Thanks."

Ryoko sulked.

When Kijou had first taken out the shades, Ryoko had been convinced he was *trying* to look like a yakuza. Once they were on, though, his look changed dramatically: He suddenly became kind of stylish, like someone from a movie, like one of the *Men in Black*.

"I really meant it," she muttered.

Aki sighed. "Honestly, Ryoko. We're going to try and save Kyo. It might be dangerous. You do know that, right?"

"Yeah . . ." Ryoko trailed off. She knew that, but she couldn't help thinking about other things. Ryoko didn't think her comment had been that off-topic, anyway.

Utsume had once told her she was "a source of unexpected ideas." He might not have meant it as a compliment, but the

memory was enough to help her recover. Her mood could turn on a dime like that.

Aki had called Ryoko about ten minutes ago, saying that Utsume had sent a message to Takemi's phone and that she'd called Kijou, who was going to accompany them to the school.

"He has a car. Get ready to sneak out."

This wasn't an easy task. Ryoko had begged her roommate for help, though, and she'd managed to escape. When she reached the road, the black car had been waiting. Aki already was inside, and they'd be at school in ten minutes. The girls' dorm was farther from school than the boys'.

The car was headed to school now.

"Um, Kijou?" Ryoko asked, leaning forward.

"What?"

"Do we really . . . have to fight Ayame?"

"Yes. We have no choice," Kijou answered.

"Oh," Ryoko sighed. She'd expected this. She was sorry, especially where Utsume was concerned. Still, she couldn't help but feel sympathy for Ayame.

She knew Ayame had spirited away Utsume, and Ryoko knew she would miss the Dark Prince . . . yet, oddly enough, Ryoko couldn't bring herself to blame Ayame. That last glimpse of Ayame's face was stuck in her mind. No matter how good the actress, no one could produce an expression that heartbreaking—it had to be real. And her expression had made it seem as if Ayame were about to abandon everything she held dear.

What had that meant? Ryoko hadn't made up her mind.

"You feel sorry for her, Kusakabe?" Kijou asked.

"Yeah," Ryoko answered honestly.

Kijou grinned at her in the rearview mirror. "Nice of you. I won't tell you not to worry, but the truth is that we don't know how to exterminate—how to kill her."

"Eh?" Ryoko said, taken aback. Come to think of it, he'd said something similar in the hospital.

"All we can do is drive her away," he continued, "snatching Kyoichi Utsume from her clutches. If one lays hands on a monster, it is the human who winds up hurt."

"Really?" Ryoko said, head to one side. She kind of understood.

"Yep," Kijou said, embarrassed. "I'm going to make her give up on Utsume. But I'm not going to do anything to her; I *can't* do anything to her. All we can do is safely return Utsume to the human side of things and make her go back to having no human contact. That's all. Does that make you feel any better?"

"Yeah, I guess—a little," Ryoko said. It wasn't that easy, really, but she didn't want Kijou to feel useless.

That left her with a different question, though. "Um, so driving her away without hurting her . . . how, exactly?" Ryoko asked.

"Oh, um," Kijou started.

Before he could finish, Aki, who had been staring out the window with a bored expression this whole time, suddenly interrupted him: "Sorry, would you stop the car?"

"Why?" Kijou asked, frowning.

"A friend," Aki answered, pointing back down the sidewalk in the direction they'd come.

Ryoko recognized the boy running down the sidewalk, out of breath. "Takemi? Why?"

"He's involved in this?" Kijou asked.

"Um, yes. He is."

"Okay," and Kijou stopped the car at once. There were no other cars, so he quickly backed up toward Takemi.

Aki opened the window, poking out her head. "Kondou, what are you doing?" she said.

Ryoko looked out, as well. "Yoo-hoo, Takemi!"

Takemi stopped, looking almost as guilty as he did exhausted.

"Wh-whose car?" He panted, changing the subject.

"It belongs to the ghost hunters. We're on our way to take out a certain ghost girl. You?"

"Eh? Um, I was, uh . . ." Takemi stammered, deliberately avoiding Aki's eyes.

"You were what?" she prompted.

"Eh? Oh, um, yeah. I . . . oh, just take me with you!" he said, flinging caution to the wind.

Aki sighed. "I told you to stay where you were."

"Aki! That's so mean!"

"Argh. Kijou, what do you think?" Aki asked.

Kijou turned around. "Fine with me. Get in. You've come this far, we might as well get everyone in the same place."

He pushed the button on the door, and the passenger door unlocked. Aki jerked her head, and Takemi climbed in. The car sped away quietly.

For a few minutes, the only sound in the car was Takemi catching his breath.

"You okay, Takemi?" Ryoko asked, concerned.

Still feeling a little guilty for disobeying orders, Takemi just nodded.

Ryoko thought Aki was the one out of line, so Takemi should relax. But that's just the way Takemi was. Ryoko rather liked this weakness in his personality; she thought it was cute.

"So, everyone's coming," Ryoko said.

"I guess I'm not surprised," Aki said, giving up. They were only a few hundred yards from the school. "Hurry, Kijou. Murakami should be there by now."

Kijou nodded silently.

Aki said nothing more.

Ryoko wondered how they could explain Kijou to Takemi.

Takemi still was breathing heavily.

Silence fell once more.

Unable to find words, they all sat, quiet like martyrs, lost in their thoughts and watching the school draw closer.

Two

Toshiya Murakami was running.

It was easy to get over the main gate; however, to avoid the slight risk of being caught by the night guard, he had snuck in past the mountain in back. Ever since, he had been running around, searching for Utsume.

The campus of Seisou University High School was extremely large.

It was night, so he couldn't get into the buildings; even so, there was no shortage of places to search. He couldn't call out for Utsume, so he ran like the wind in total silence.

The school was quiet: brick and concrete buildings, plenty of trees, all lit by moonlight—giving it the serenity of abandoned ruins.

He couldn't find Utsume. He couldn't find anything moving at all.

Everything was quiet, like he had slipped into some other world. No matter where he ran, the darkness continued, tinged blue by the light of the moon.

Clicking his tongue, Toshiya stopped running and looked around him.

He took a breath. Toshiya was breathing faster, but he was not out of breath; once he'd taken two or three deep breaths, his breathing returned to normal. Considering he had bolted out of the house after Takemi called, taken the bus to a stop near the school, and then run the half mile from the stop, this was extremely impressive.

He was surrounded by cherry trees. The moon was so bright that the trees, the buildings, and Toshiya all cast shadows on the ground.

He couldn't see Utsume anywhere, though.

He tightened his hands into fists. Toshiya was getting frustrated—partly because he couldn't find Utsume, mostly because ever since he'd entered the school grounds, things had been strange. Something felt wrong. The feeling was difficult to pin down, but it was making him irritable.

At first, he hadn't noticed. Not noticing, the unsettling feeling had puzzled him, annoyed him. Now, though, stopping to think—and turning his attention to the world around him—he finally figured it out: There was no sound.

It was unnaturally silent. He listened closely, searching for anything. But Toshiya was the only thing making noise anywhere. Even the leaves of the cherry trees failed to rustle.

This was well beyond the still of the night. Night was never soundless. The wind made noise, animals and insects made noise . . . The night was filled with many sounds not made by humans, especially here, in the mountains.

And yet, here, there was no sound at all. The silence was so strong that it hurt Toshiya's ears. There was a tension in the air, as if the moonlight were absorbing all the sound.

Something was wrong. Something was unnatural. Toshiya could not say what.

Is it always this way? he wondered, frowning. Even as he thought, he knew it wasn't. The serenity here could never bring peace of mind.

A *chilly* silence—that was the word for it. The whole campus was cold and quiet, bringing anxiety, chilling the soul.

He couldn't find Utsume. He was getting anxious.

"Wish I had a cell phone," Toshiya muttered.

He had planned to take the advantage and hadn't expected to be spinning his wheels like this. He hated cell phones, found them irritating; now, he was left cursing his lack of one. If he didn't hurry, Takemi or the others would catch up with him.

Toshiya started running again.

He wasn't going to waste time wishing for things he didn't have. He no longer had time to waste on idle thoughts. He had to find Utsume quickly and clear up this whole mess.

Yes. Quickly. Alone. Without anyone else getting involved.

He ran on.

He'd been all around the school. He couldn't think of anywhere else to look outside, and he couldn't get inside. Neither could Utsume, though, so Toshiya must have missed him outside. He ran around the school a second time.

Part of him already had realized the truth, though: No matter how long he ran, he never would find Utsume, because this was no longer the kind of world where an ordinary human could accomplish anything relying on his own abilities.

Ignoring this feeling, Toshiya kept running.

The moment she stood in front of the gate, Aki was enveloped by the school's unnatural quiet. Her ears rang. The ears, as receptors of sound, did not seem to function properly in a world devoid of sound.

An indescribable anxiety rose within her, and she said, "It's very quiet."

"Very quiet indeed," Kijou said, getting out of his black car in his black suit, every inch one of the men in black—the mysterious men that appeared out of nowhere anytime a person got mixed up with a UFO. He looked like a movie poster; and yet, the impression he gave off was more sinister and vivid than cool.

"Too quiet. This may be a cone of silence. Be careful," Kijou cautioned, looking around him intently.

Aki had assumed the school always was like this at night, but Kijou's tone implied otherwise.

"Cone . . . what?"

"Cone of silence—a soundless area often reported after UFO contact and the like."

The sudden mention of UFOs floored Aki. Coming from someone who could be one of the men in black, it didn't sound like a joke.

"Those who encounter a UFO claim to be surrounded by this cone of silence. Similar experiences are reported with many other types of abnormal phenomena—especially time slips or other unnatural pockets of space. People who have stepped into an unnatural place suddenly find there is no background noise, feel that the area is unnaturally quiet . . . but we know too little about it to say for certain if that is what's happening here," Kijou explained, staring around him with great interest.

Now that he had pointed it out, it did seem a little creepy the way the trees made no noise.

Ryoko stepped ahead of them. "I've never seen the school gate closed before!" she said, evidently enjoying herself. She seemed almost manic.

Next to her, Takemi was equally carefree. "It really does look different," he said.

They had informed him that Kijou's job was fighting ghosts; although it was a little ludicrous, Takemi seemed to accept it.

"Oh, a ghost hunter? I saw a show about them on TV," he had said.

Aki had assumed he meant a movie. Apparently, she was wrong.

"You've never heard of them? They're the people that bring in cameras and sensors and instruments where a poltergeist has been. I saw some people from England . . ."

Now that he mentioned it, it did ring a bell—weren't those scientists, though?

"Let's go," Kijou said, bringing Aki back to Earth.

"Oh, right," she said, chiding herself for getting lost in thought. This was no time for that.

They approached the gate. *Now what?* she thought.

Kijou opened it easily, though—it hadn't been locked.

Everyone looked surprised.

"Oh, we cleared things with the guards. No matter what we do tonight, none of them will show up."

This "Agency" Kijou worked for was a lot more powerful than Aki had imagined.

Kijou opened the gate wide enough for a person to pass and slipped inside. Then, he beckoned them after him. "Hurry."

Everyone looked at one another, nodded, and followed him inside, one by one.

Kijou placed his hand on the gate again. As silently as possible, he closed it behind them.

Three

Beyond the main gate at the south, the Seisou High campus could be divided roughly into two parts: To the west were the school buildings, and to the east was everything else.

Even discounting sports fields and the pool, the east side of campus was far larger. Club buildings, the martial arts hall, the library . . . and between those buildings, the grounds were laid out like a park. This part of the campus had been designed with an eye toward eventual expansion. Once benches were placed all around, though, the students made use of it just as it was. It was the complete opposite of the school building area, where everything was packed tightly together.

There were a lot of cherry trees on the east side. What the idea had been, no one knew—but there were a ridiculously large number of them.

Takemi led the group along, past the fading blossoms. Clouds of petals drifted through the air. In the moonlight, they turned both sky and ground white. Takemi thought it was beautiful—perhaps too beautiful. It was beyond unreal. It seemed steeped in madness.

It reminded him of that famous novel by Sakaguchi Ango, *Beneath the Cherry Trees in Full Bloom*. It was that kind of beautiful, silent world that makes all who see it tremble.

Stomping down a strange sort of restlessness inside themselves, they all walked on, beneath the cherry trees. Utsume might be there. Utsume's message was their only clue: *"school cherry."*

Takemi had a hunch where. Behind the club building, under the cherry trees, there was a bench that Utsume often used. If Utsume mentioned cherry trees, that was what they all thought of.

"That's strange, where . . . ?" Takemi said, at a loss. He'd looked all over behind the club building, but he couldn't find the bench.

It wasn't there.

Aki and Ryoko were frowning, too. It should have been right here, right behind the club building.

Everyone remembered that it was here. However, the exact location seemed to elude them. No matter how much they searched, they couldn't find it. They were walking around under the cherry trees, around and around, feeling as if they were covering the same ground again and again.

They all were stymied by the puzzling cobwebs in their memory. It was like the place they were headed had been pulled out of their minds—and out of reality.

Kijou said nothing. He simply nodded, showing that he didn't doubt them.

They kept looking, frantic. And it wasn't long before their search led them to Toshiya.

Hearing footsteps, Takemi turned, and his eyes met Toshiya's.

"Takemi?" Toshiya said grimly.

He'd heard them and followed the noise. He hadn't found Utsume yet, either.

Hearing them talking, Ryoko joined them. "What's going on? Did you find the Dark Prince?"

Everyone else came out, as well. Toshiya looked at them in surprise. "Why are you here?"

He wasn't surprised to see Takemi after him, but Aki, Ryoko and a man he didn't know? That was unexpected.

"We came to say, 'hi,'" Aki said sarcastically.

Takemi brought him up to speed, hoping Toshiya could help. "His Majesty said 'cherry' in the message. And if he says 'cherry,' then that means the bench, right? So we're all looking for it, but we can't find it. None of us can remember where it is. . . ."

Toshiya listened with a strained expression, having forgotten about the bench himself.

"What do you mean you don't—" Then, he stared into space for a moment before shaking his head. "Oh, right. My memory is strangely hazy, as well. I can remember that he had a favorite bench, but I can't remember where I was when I saw him on it. If I saw it, I'm sure I'd recognize it, though."

"Yep, same as the rest of us."

All three had said much the same thing. The place had been hidden, Takemi was sure of it.

Toshiya's interest already had turned elsewhere. "So?" he said, shifting his gaze.

"What?"

"Who is he?" he said, regarding Kijou with suspicion.

The only adult, the only outsider—who was he, what was he doing here?

Kijou grinned, not bothered at all.

"This man fights ghosts," Aki said. "He was my lead. He's helping for free, says he knows a way to drive away that ghost girl."

"My name's Kijou. You must be Murakami. Nice to meet you."

"Yeah," Toshiya said, accepting him for the time being. Neither bowed.

Toshiya remained on his guard, and Takemi could have sworn that he saw their bodies tense, that they were keeping a safe distance from each other. This might have been his imagination, though, an impression caused by the air of tension Toshiya always gave off.

There was a long silence.

Aki interrupted it. "Okay, then. So, Murakami, what did your lead turn up?"

Murakami said nothing. He looked like he was trying to make up his mind how to answer. Takemi was doing the same. How could he possibly explain about their meeting with Jinno?

Nothing he had said or done had made much sense. Then, Takemi remembered something: the bell.

Ring came a sound in his ears. He couldn't believe it. Here, in the silent, moonlit cherry grove, he had heard a faint bell ring.

It was that bell, but he had not heard it directly—only its echo.

"I can hear the bell!" Takemi said, taking a step forward. Everyone stopped talking and stared at him in surprise.

"What do you mean, Takemi?" Ryoko asked, worried.

Takemi turned his back, listening closely, searching for the direction.

Ring. It came again.

"This way," he said, stepping toward a small clearing in the cherry trees. Everyone stared at him, unnerved, making no effort to move.

The echo was coming from that direction. It was very faint and delicate—but if he listened closely, he could tell where it was coming from.

"The bell! Can't you hear it?" Takemi said.

Ring.

No one said anything. Now, it was Takemi's turn to look spooked.

"Wait, no one can hear that?"

Ryoko hesitated before shaking her head. "No."

Takemi felt a shiver run down his spine, like he'd just stepped into a cold shower.

Ring.

"There it is again!" Takimi said. Even he thought his voice sounded like he was on the verge of tears. He turned to run back to the others, but Toshiya stopped him.

"That's it! Find it, Kondou!"

"Huh?"

"It's the magician's bell! If he wasn't a total fraud, then that noise is where Utsume is!"

"Oh!" Fear had stopped him from thinking. It seemed so obvious.

The other three looked puzzled.

Takemi's hands trembled as he took the bell out of his pocket. It hung from his cell phone, looking just as it always had. It made no sound at all. For reasons Takemi didn't understand, though, he *knew* the bell was causing this sound.

"W-why me? You were the one he talked to!" Takemi said, flummoxed.

"You're the one who took it. Whoever touches it first owns it!" Toshiya replied. Takemi made no further protests.

Ring. The sound came again.

"Murakami, I'm very close to it! What should I do?"

"I don't know! If you can't see it, grab it!"

"Really?"

Takemi gingerly reached out both hands, stepping toward the sound.

Ring . . . ring . . .

The sound grew closer.

"Eek!" Something caught at his foot. Unfathomable anxiety squeezed his heart. He was trying to move forward, but his feet were withering—as if he were in a dream, running but getting nowhere. If he hadn't heard the bell again, he never could've moved forward. But he did hear it, and he forced himself forward. Like in a dream, his body moved like he was underwater. He wasn't moving at all. Panic rose within him, about to explode.

And then, the world turned inside out.

His body felt real again. The landscape twisted into something almost exactly like what he had been looking at before, yet somehow very different. His heart still beat quickly; however, it was from the relief of knowing that everything had passed. His trembling and shaking subsided quickly.

He could feel it. This strange, otherworldly feeling was very remote, yet oddly familiar. It was just like . . . waking up.

Just as before, a clearing in the cherry trees.

Blossoms on the trees and ground turned everything white.

Petals drifting down from above.

Melting into the white below, spreading the whiteness on the ground.

A blue bench.

A couple sitting on the bench.

The boy in black, holding a cell phone.

The girl in dark red, singing.

The song, resonant.

"People are real,
Ayakashi are dreams,
The heart a boundary,
Blood a bond.
Everything is where it should be.
Red sky to red earth.
The moon and sun must return to the horizon,
So let us hope they do.
Children must return to their parents,
So let us hope they do.
Separated on the border,
Awakened from the dream,

Returned to reality,
The children come home.
The bonds of flesh draw them,
Out of the dream, back to reali—"

The song cut off.

Takemi remembered himself.

Ayame was looking at him. Her eyes registered surprise, relief, and acceptance—and a parade of other emotions that Takemi could not even guess.

Utsume looked up, saw Takemi, and said, "You're in time." He snapped his cell phone closed.

He gave Takemi a look almost as if he were impressed. Then—and this was unbelievably strange for him—he gave a sigh of relief.

"Sorry," he said.

And in that one word, Takemi understood: They had been correct to come here. Utsume had not wanted to disappear.

"Your Majesty." He could feel tears welling up, and feelings he couldn't put words to filled his chest. Indescribable emotions buffeted him. And the flow of them reversed and exploded when Takemi saw the girl sitting next to Utsume, the cause of all this misfortune. He reached out for Ayame. "All because of *you!*"

"I'm sorry! I'm sorry!"

He grabbed her roughly by the collar.

She let out a tiny shriek, turning her face away from Takemi's glare like she'd been slapped.

"I'm sorry, I'm sorry," Ayame apologized, crying. She didn't look like anything but a frail girl. That wasn't enough to stop Takemi's anger, though.

Utsume was taken by *this?*

Utsume almost had disappeared forever. That fact suddenly felt very real to Takemi. This abrupt realization of the danger gave him goose bumps.

He shouted, "Why? Why Utsume? Why my friend? Why did you have to take my friend? Why does someone this incredible have to disappear?"

Unconsciously, his hands tightened their grip on her.

Her face twisted in pain. Still, she apologized. Despite the pressure on her throat, she kept whispering, "I'm sorry," hoarsely, begging for forgiveness.

Takemi tightened his grip still more.

"Stop, Kondou," Utsume said, grabbing Takemi's wrist.

"Don't stop me!"

"Fine," Utsume said, emotionless. "What are you planning? Are you going to hit her? Strangle her to death?"

This cooled Takemi's head a little. He'd grabbed her out of anger, without thinking things through. *Hit her? Strangle her?* These shocking words didn't sound like things he could do.

Face twisting, he let her go.

Freed, Ayame began coughing.

When he saw that, Utsume at last let go of Takemi's arm.

Takemi glared up at Utsume. "Your Majesty . . ."

"Sorry. This is the result of what I desired. If you must bear a grudge, bear it against me," Utsume said.

As he spoke, he glanced toward the coughing Ayame. "This was an experiment. I theorized that it might be possible to bring a kami-kakushi back to our side. She was against the idea the entire time—and yes, I was naive. I did everything I could think of, resisted her as best I could . . . but I started to vanish after only sixty hours. I never expected the other world to penetrate so quickly."

He stood there calmly analyzing the way he nearly had disappeared forever: "I did not plan to vanish without a fight . . . or was it that I didn't care what happened?"

Takemi had no answer. This man was much too indifferent about his own death.

Utsume looked up. "What did I really want?"

To Takemi, Utsume looked as if he were regretting not having vanished.

"Looks like we're in time," Kijou muttered.

Ryoko tore her eyes away from them. She couldn't speak. She couldn't understand what she had just witnessed. Before her was the bench they had been unable to find, along with Utsume and Ayame.

Takemi had done . . . something. And then, suddenly, there had been a bright flash, and the fog that had been clouding her vision and memories seemed to have cleared away.

What was that? Ryoko shuffled through her memories.

Takemi had said something about hearing a bell, and then he had an incomprehensible conversation with Toshiya before beginning to walk toward an empty area. . . . That was all.

"What . . . was that?"

Aki and Toshiya both looked dazed, as if they'd seen an amazing trick—or even genuine magic.

"*That* is a kami-kakushi," Kijou said. "Legends of them have been in Hazama for centuries. We don't know when they began,

exactly, but we do know that they occurred regularly until at least the early years of the Showa era. For the last fifty years, there has been nothing—but *that* is what this girl is. She is *one of them*."

Ryoko could see Takemi grabbing Ayame's collar. Kijou continued his explanation as if nothing were happening, but Ryoko's attention was torn between the two of them, and she grew confused.

"Eh?"

"So, this is an extremely unusual case. As far as I know, there is no prior example. Recovery from a kami-kakushi—a direct encounter—and this bell, all in one night. Remarkable. What a night."

"Um, Kijou?"

"The kami-kakushi legend, the ghost girl in the school, and the kami-kakushi incident eleven years ago—they all come together here. The efforts of the information bureau were not in vain. Now, this is my job."

Aki asked pointedly, "Come together? What are you—"

"They . . . No, I'll explain later," Kijou said, changing his mind. Ryoko thought she heard a slight tremor in his voice. He was extremely tense. He had been talking to calm himself down.

"Um . . ."

She was about to ask if he was okay, but she froze instead. Kijou had taken a gun out of his jacket and calmly pointed it at Ayame.

He's really going to do it! she thought. She could feel her chest tighten.

Kijou said quietly, "Preparing to eliminate. Nobody move."

Kijou's face had turned cold in an instant.

Ryoko closed her eyes.

Then, she heard the heavy sound of something being hit, followed by a sharp whistle of something tearing through the air. There was a man's groan.

Timidly opening her eyes, she saw Kijou, clutching his hand. He had dropped the gun, and Toshiya stood in front of him, ready to fight. The two figures were glaring at each other.

"Uh . . . what?" Ryoko said, confused. *What is going on?*

Face strained with pain, Kijou smiled. "You didn't need to kick me! What's your problem?"

Toshiya said nothing, simply continuing to stare down at him grimly, alert to any move on Kijou's part. You could see the caution in his eyes.

Ryoko asked, "What, Murakami?"

Toshiya didn't answer. Instead, keeping his eyes on Kijou, he asked, "You were aiming at Utsume, weren't you?"

Kijou didn't answer. The smile on his lips was altogether different from before.

○ ○ ○

Four

"Why?" Aki quietly asked Kijou.

It wasn't that she hadn't been rattled. She was just shy of panic, probably. She looked completely calm, though. She was accustomed to keeping her cool. It was second nature. She did not show others weakness.

Even if it didn't show, Aki was shaken. She was conflicted, anguished—and pretty much any other word for having turbulent emotions raging inside you. The man she had brought to save Utsume was trying to kill him instead.

Given the shift in circumstances, what should she do? She was conflicted. And because her actions had put Utsume in danger, she was anguished.

And . . . when Kijou had taken aim, she'd felt a dark sort of glee and relief inside. It had its roots in jealousy. She might've been insisting she was trying to save Utsume; in truth, though, Aki had been working out of jealousy and hatred of Ayame.

A tar made of self-loathing seemed to be burning inside Aki, turning her heart to cinders. Her own deceit and weakness brought Aki to despair. This internal conflict gave an edge to her expression, but she just stood there, looking quietly furious.

"Why?"

No matter the consequences, Aki's ego would not permit her to back down now. This was her last vestige of pride.

"Necessary measures," Kijou said, carefully stepping backward, moving away from the gun he'd dropped. He didn't look at it. He was abandoning the gun, focusing on Toshiya. If he tried to pick it up, Toshiya would attack.

Kijou's natural poise had a frightening quality to it that Aki understood. It was like the sense of ease that a seasoned fighter has, but it was boiled down to a syrup. The total lack of fear in a combat situation makes the opponent feel fear, instead.

"Yes, this is a necessary measure," Kijou said again.

"Killing Kyo?"

"Exactly."

"Why?"

"Because Utsume's existence is what brought the kami-kakushi here."

Aki's expression stiffened.

Kijou smiled, an oddly friendly smile that was out of place. "I explained the process by which these beings enter our world, right? A person susceptible to the paranormal infected by a ghost story—a person who *knows*—allows them to be here. Did you think it was strange? That you could see her, too?

"It's because Utsume is acting as a host, 'sharing' her existence with the rest of you. His susceptibility acts as a channel, allowing you to see her. Even I can see her. Shared through you to me. Do you see? Right now, he is the broadcast point, taking her from the other world and transmitting that world to us, like a radio tower or a network server. Just as panic can spread through a crowd, she will continue to spread if we do nothing."

"So what?"

"*We all are in danger.* At any time, if the conditions are right, we could become her victims. And those candidates will increase—soon, there will be a torrent of disappearances.

"There's a way out. *We* are not susceptible; we are receiving transmitted information. If we take out the source of that information, then all the information we have received will vanish, and we will be ordinary humans once more. This is my job: reducing the number of victims of the other world, as much as I possibly can."

"So *what*, exactly, do you want to do?" Aki's voice shook with emotion.

Kijou sighed. "Someone as smart as you must already know by now: I will dispose of Utsume, and then I'll take a few psychological measures against the rest of you to make you forget what happened. And that will, while minimizing casualties, safely drive that creature from this world.

"Utsume will be a tragic victim of an accident. This will prevent the creation of another 'real ghost story,' which would bring these beings back, causing more people to fall prey to the paranormal. If it got out that Utsume was taken by a kami-kakushi, then that would start another story, which eventually would trickle down to someone who could call the kami-kakushi forth again. At the moment, *this* is the most efficient method we have of dealing with them."

Kijou continued, "To protect the greatest number of people, including all of you, we must sacrifice Utsume. It is very sad, but there is no other way. At the least, we have come a long way since the days of the witch hunts. This is happening all over the world. No exceptions allowed. Do you understand that?"

Without a second's pause, Toshiya said, "No."

"Then, you will have to use force," Kijou said matter-of-factly.

Ryoko was right next to Kijou, and she began edging backward. "I-I'll go get help!"

"Ah! Idiot!"

Too late. No sooner had the words left her mouth than Kijou employed an *atemi* strike against her. His elbow slammed into her solar plexus, and she folded up.

Toshiya stepped forward, but Kijou was prepared for that, using his elbow to swing Ryoko around and fling her at Toshiya.

Her head was down; if she landed on it, she would be badly hurt. Toshiya had no choice but to catch her. This gave Kijou time to gain some distance.

"Close one. You're faster than I thought. Strong, and with good judgment. Young people today are scary!" Kijou said flippantly. It was hard to tell if he meant it or not.

"Is Ryoko okay?" Aki asked.

Lowering the unconscious girl to the ground, Toshiya nodded.

Aki looked relieved. Ryoko's life was in no danger.

Kijou said, "Once the first to be infected is determined, the treatment regulations are beyond question. If you behave yourselves, we will not treat you poorly. Stop fighting, please."

Aki turned toward him, refusal in her eyes.

"Darn," Kijou murmured, not looking at all put out.

Suddenly, the ground near Takemi spurted upward.

A moment later, he realized someone had shot at him; by that time, the fight already had begun.

Toshiya and Kijou were glaring at each other. On the ground beside them was a pistol with a silencer—a kind he'd seen a lot in video games. He was pretty sure it was called a SOCOM pistol, and it was bigger than he would've expected. Its presence seemed out of place in this world, and it took Takemi a moment to grasp the reality of the situation. When he finally did, he shuddered. That gun apparently had been pointed at Utsume.

While this was going on, Kijou struck Ryoko and threw her. While Takemi gaped uselessly, the situation was growing worse.

"Stop fighting, please," he could just make out Kijou's cold invitation to surrender.

By that time, all the blood had drained from his face.

"Run, Your Majesty! He's going to kill you!" Takemi almost shrieked.

He forced his spinning brain to think. They outnumbered Kijou. They might be able to buy enough time for Utsume to run.

"Hurry!"

Utsume didn't move, though. He was watching the action unfolding around him, expressionless.

Takemi panicked. "What are you doing? He's trying to kill you!"

"Apparently."

"Right! So, why aren't you running?"

"It would be pointless."

"Why?"

"Even if I run, they'll find me soon. There are only so many places a high school student can go. The best thing to do is settle this here."

"But . . ."

Takemi wanted to say something about not knowing if you didn't try. However, the emotionless way Utsume spoke suggested that he was hardly in the mood for optimism.

"But . . . but . . . you'll die!" he managed. He had no idea what he was trying to say.

Utsume's expression shifted slightly: His eyes went out of focus, as if he were reminiscing while staring into the distance. "Oh, that's fine with me."

A chill ran down Takemi's spine. The horrible emptiness in Utsume's voice, in his expression, seemed to grab Takemi's heart and squeeze. For a moment, Takemi felt like he was talking to someone who already was dead.

There was a struggle between life and death within Utsume; each tortured him equally. Deep down, he longed for both.

Looking sad, Ayame leaned up against him, like a banshee heralding death.

"Your Majesty . . ." Takemi groaned, powerless.

The two of them were so beautiful. There was no one in the world better suited to be by Utsume's side at that moment.

Against that hollow beauty of the other world, Takemi felt horribly isolated.

While he stared at Utsume, he heard Toshiya kick the ground.

There would be no negotiating. The moment he was sure of that, Toshiya moved—one step forward into range. Tightening his fist, he swung hard for the man's face.

This was no official match, with rules and patterns. It was simply a fight wherein it would be very hard to dodge the opponent's blows.

Kijou was concentrating on his defense, staying on guard. He caught Toshiya's blow, deflecting it and, in one smooth motion, striking Toshiya's body with his other hand.

Toshiya twisted his body, absorbing the damage.

Still off balance, they crashed together, grappling.

Toshiya's uncle had not taught him proper karate. Although his uncle was a professional karate instructor, Toshiya was not ranked and had never been in a tournament. He knew only the fundamentals of karate. This was what Toshiya had wanted.

His uncle, a rather unusual person, had gone on a warrior's journey in the hopes of becoming a great fighter. He had been in more fights than just about anybody. So, instead of training Toshiya in karate, his uncle had taught him the basics of every form of martial arts he knew, and they had spent the rest of their time sparring. They

probably had spent far more time grappling than they had practicing the *kata*. Toshiya had been injured many times, knocked out even more—but when he fought, he was not bound to the kata.

Toshiya had been hoping they would grapple. He was a full head taller than Kijou. If he could take advantage of that, he could stop him here, keeping him away from Utsume. Ideally, he wanted to keep Kijou pinned down.

Kijou did not use any direct force. He seemed to be well aware that he had a physical disadvantage, so he held his ground with as little force as possible, inviting Toshiya to go on the offensive.

Presumably, Kijou had some wrestling moves up his sleeves. Guessing this, Toshiya avoided any of Kijou's attempts to overpower him. Their arms locked together, he kneed Kijou in the belly.

"Unh!"

The impact wasn't strong enough. Kijou had shifted backward, and the blow was shallow. Toshiya quickly tried to land a second hit . . . and lost his balance.

Just before the leg Toshiya had raised to knee Kijou hit the ground, Kijou dropped his body, squatting down and sweeping Toshiya's other leg out from under him.

His height advantage now turned against him, Toshiya's upper body was yanked downward, his body sent flying in a kind of *tomoe-nage*. He landed well. It was far from a finishing blow, but the distance it placed between them hurt.

Toshiya got to his feet.

Kijou was up already, keeping a careful distance.

They were back to square one. Toshiya cursed under his breath: Kijou clearly had more fighting experience than Toshiya.

They faced off in the basic *hanmi* fighting stance.

As they glared at each other, Kijou said, "Society is formed through the disposal of harmful substances."

Toshiya frowned at him.

"Society is a fragile thing. Anytime humans draw together, some form of society arises, but that society is destined to shatter when exposed to the least bit of stress. It's a result of human nature. A bubble that is too big, too fragile—that's what society is."

Toshiya said nothing.

"Humans need society. It isn't always correct, though—tragically, sometimes blameless individuals become enemies of society. Crime, dangerous animals, diseases, thoughts, and other societies . . . in some cases, these elements are nothing more than scapegoats.

"Regardless, society must be protected. Few humans are able to survive without it. We punish criminals, quarantine the sick, drive away dangerous animals—if we do not protect society this way, many people will be unhappy. Society succeeds only because of the average person in it."

Slowly, Kijou added, "Right now, Utsume is a carrier with a deadly disease. As part of a public health agency, I can't overlook his condition. We must prevent the spread of the other world, we must prevent her existence from becoming public knowledge.

"Someone has to do it. Not only society is at risk—your lives are in danger, as well. We must isolate the disease carrier. The carrier's death will protect our world. None of you are stupid. Won't you give him to me?"

This was Kijou's final warning. His attitude revealed that they weren't getting another chance.

"To hell with that," Toshiya spat. "If the world's going to end unless Utsume dies, then let it end."

"A pity. You are now the enemy of mankind," Kijou said, narrowing his eyes.

Screw it, Toshiya thought. Sure, what Kijou was saying probably was right, even just. Toshiya didn't give a damn about that, though.

Toshiya had chosen to be normal. "Normal" implied neither good nor bad, his uncle had said. "Good" meant killing yourself for other people, and "bad" meant killing other people for yourself. Now, Toshiya was trying to kill someone for someone else. This was what his uncle meant by "normal."

"I will not let anyone hurt my friend," Toshiya announced.

Kijou nodded, "I agree. My 'friend' is the greater number of people."

As he spoke, he launched an attack, quickly slipping up within reach.

Toshiya stood his ground. Kijou took another step forward, into his range, and Toshiya put the full force of his body behind a side kick.

The fight was over in a second.

Kijou had no time to dodge, and the kick struck him hard in the side.

Toshiya had used his joints well, putting enough weight behind his kick, and it slammed into Kijou's body.

Kijou took the full force of the blow and fell over, groaning.

The fight was over.

Toshiya fell to his knees.

Kijou slowly stood back up. "That hurt a lot," he said, out of breath. "I didn't want to spend much time on this, so I had no choice. I think you cracked a rib through the guard, but I can fight still. You can't, though, can you?" Kijou wiped the trickle of blood spilling out of his mouth with his sleeve.

Toshiya said nothing. The sweat pouring down his face said everything his voice did not.

In that instant, Toshiya had broken his ankle.

Aware of the size difference, Kijou had avoided a long fight. He had taken Toshiya's kick, grabbed the leg with his body, and used the force of the blow, the weight behind it, to destroy Toshiya's kicking leg: a sacrifice move. To stop Toshiya's leg like that took as much precision as it did nerve.

"As long as you can't move, I can take out the rest, even injured," Kijou said, slowly moving away. Even now that Toshiya had lost the use of his legs, Kijou was taking no chances.

Toshiya gritted his teeth. If Kijou had moved in to finish him off, Toshiya would have had any number of ways to turn the tables. However, Kijou was headed toward Utsume to finish him off instead. There was no way for Toshiya to get near Kijou, much less attack.

"Don't worry. You will forget everything that happens here and return to your old lives. Utsume will have died in an accident. You will have no reason to question that. And that will be all. Anyone can die when his cards are up. Of course, it's sad; eventually, though, the sadness will fade. High school students die every day, all over the world. Utsume's death will be one such instance.

"Nobody imagines that his friends will die today or tomorrow. Death comes to us all, though. Everyone whose friend has died recovers from the grief, and so your sorrow will heal in time. Stop fighting me, and I won't have to hurt you," Kijou said in persuasive tones.

Toshiya ignored him, trying to think of a plan. Nothing sprang to mind. He was breathing heavily. The pain from his broken ankle was about to put him in shock.

He forced his brain to think.

Kijou probably had known exactly what Toshiya was doing. His face had softened into a lonely smile, one that looked out of place with his features. It was a strange expression. Now that Toshiya thought about it, reluctantly refusing to stop lecturing them even after his final warning was a little odd, as well.

It was possible that Kijou had a high opinion of them, that it made him sad to hurt them. Maybe he was seeking their forgiveness?

Kijou continued, "You are all young and strong. For your age, you have astonishing strength of will and morality. And knowledge. I've enjoyed meeting all of you. I don't want to hurt you. Will you please—"

Kijou's words suddenly cut off. He spun around.

Someone was moving. Aki had dashed over to the gun Kijou had dropped. Seeing as much, Toshiya's mind snapped back to life.

"Kidono! Don't!" he cried.

From that distance, she would be able to get the gun and point it at him before Kijou could reach her. But when they had been grappling, Toshiya had felt a lump of iron under Kijou's vest.

A terrible expression crossed Kijou's face. Regardless, he pulled out his other gun, pointing it at Aki.

There was a muffled crack as the bullet left the silencer.

Five

Just as Aki aimed the gun at Kijou, a hot wind shot past her head: It was the bullet from his warning shot speeding by. She knew it before she saw the gun Kijou had pointed at her.

If he had wanted, she would be dead right now.

A wave of incredible fear washed over her; even so, she did not let go of the gun. Her aim shook a little, but her powerful logic circuits quickly set to work, diluting her emotions. In a moment, the shaking stopped. She hadn't ever used a gun before, but she fixed the aim at Kijou's chest, where she stood the best chance of hitting something.

The girl and the man glared at each other, each holding the same kind of gun. For Kijou, the gun was like an extension of his arm; in Aki's hands, it looked massive, jarringly out of place.

"This is pointless. The recoil from a .45 is too strong for a high school girl. This is a very big, heavy gun, and your little hands can't hold it steady. Let's be generous and say you have a fifty percent chance of hitting my body; by the time the bullet hits me, I will have shot you in the head," Kijou said coldly.

Aki was sure he was right. After all, he had positioned that warning shot to fly right past her head. And Kijou was a trained fighter, so he knew to stand sideways—making himself a poor target.

Kijou was a pro. Aki had no chance against him. Still, Aki was not going to give up, not now.

"I am perfectly calm. I'd say I have a ninety percent chance. Please, Kijou. Give up and go home. If you're hit in the torso by a .45, you won't be able to shake that off. Can you win then—even if you shoot me in the head? Murakami may be injured, but you'd have to contend with Kondou and Kyo, too—all three of them fighting you," she said, bottling up her fear.

It took a huge amount of strength for her to speak those words. The fear generated by the gun pointed at her defied description. It struck the very bottom of her heart.

"I'm pretty sure I can," Kijou said quietly. "Once you have pointed a gun at me, I must consider that action an obstruction of duty, and I will try to kill you in all seriousness. What you are doing now is beyond the acceptable limits of behavior. You have ten seconds. If you do not lower the gun, I will kill you."

Aki could receive no more obvious a warning than that. A cold sweat ran down her brow.

"Okay. One . . . two . . ."

Aki hesitated. The pressure was so great she couldn't breathe, couldn't make up her mind.

"Three . . . four . . ."

Aki tried to think. Her heart beat like a drum roll, scattering her thoughts.

"Five . . . six . . ."

What should I do? she thought.

"Seven . . . eight . . ."

What was death, really?

"Nine . . ."

He was almost finished counting. Her mind went blank.

"Ten."

The moment she heard the word, Aki pulled the trigger.

Kijou didn't fire.

When the bullet hit him, a sensation like ice-cold electricity ran through his entire body. He shivered violently, and then the wound grew hot. The pain paralyzed his right arm. It would take quite some time before he could move it freely.

Kijou cursed his own weakness.

Concentrating all his will on staying conscious, he ran toward Aki, kicking the gun out of her hands.

Dazed from the shock of having shot someone, she didn't move.

He glanced at her to make sure she would not act; then, he took the gun from his immobile right hand, shifting it to his left and pointing it at Utsume. His aim trembled.

"Ack!" He had expected it: He couldn't hold the gun steady.

Four cracked ribs, organ damage, and now the bullet hole in his shoulder all made it very hard for him to aim with his off hand. It took several seconds before he calmed down. He was on edge.

I've blown this. I must complete the mission, even if it kills me.

Kijou Yutaka was a hunter agent. All his attention was on his mission.

It was true that he liked these kids. And he certainly was interested in this boy, Kyoichi Utsume, who had collected such intelligent people around him. He did not deny that he felt sympathy for the grief they would experience once he had killed Kyoichi Utsume.

None of that mattered, though. His mission remained.

Kyoichi Utsume had survived a kami-kakushi incident ten years ago. And once someone had encountered a being from the other world, it was highly likely they would do so again—that's why the Agency watched them so carefully.

And now, Utsume had done just that.

Kami-kakushi-type beings were extremely dangerous; if he blew this, there was a good chance that girl Utsume was with would claim many more victims. Failure was unacceptable. If he failed, where could he go? There was nowhere for Kijou to go besides the Agency.

Resolution steadied his hands. Concentration stopped the world from spinning. Hold your breath, aim, and fire.

"No!" Toshiya screamed.

Kijou could no longer hear him. At the other end of his gun, Utsume seemed to be appreciating some unknown irony. He betrayed no emotion, as if he didn't care if he died here. This time, Kijou pulled the trigger: Bright red blood sprang forth like a flower.

Ryoko blearily opened her eyes.

Her head and vision seemed out of focus. Sleepily, she looked around at the cherry trees. This was her school. She was on the school grounds.

Ryoko wondered why she had been sleeping there. She couldn't quite work out if she was dreaming. Her body felt extremely heavy. She didn't want to get up. So heavy. Maybe this was pain? A heavy, dull pain? Ryoko didn't much care.

Everything around her was white, the cherry blossoms making it even more so, as if a white mist covered everything. People were moving through that mist. Ryoko watched them.

Her eyes were still half-dreaming, and the figures weren't solid. She couldn't work out what they were doing. There was one figure she could see clearly, though.

Oh, Ayame's here. . . . .

Ryoko watched her absently. The girl in the red cape was standing there, with an air of desperation. She looked so pretty.

Her lips, the color of cherry blossoms, were taut. Ryoko stared at Ayame's beautiful, earnest expression as her mind sluggishly began to work.

What are you thinking?

What are you feeling?

What does that face mean?

"Oh, this," came her father's voice, a memory drifting up from her dreams.

"Oh, this. Ryoko, this is a picture of your mother before you were born. You're inside her."

"Huh."

"When we first found out she was pregnant, your mother was very sick. The doctor said if we had you, Ryoko, then your mother might die."

"Oh?"

"Everyone told your mother she shouldn't have you. We already had your sister, Satoko, so we didn't need any more children, they said. I agreed with them, at the time. I didn't want to risk your mother's life. I said we should forget about the baby.

"'Forget about the baby,' I said. 'If you die, who will look after Satoko? Isn't Satoko more important than an unborn child?'"

"And what did Mommy say?"

"Your mother glared at me, furious.

"'This is a life. A new life is forming inside me. As long as this child is alive, even if she is not yet born, she is the same as Satoko, no different. If bearing this child kills me, then I won't regret it.'

"When I heard that, I started crying.

"So, I made up my mind, as well. Knowing it might be her last, I took this picture of your mother. Look at her—doesn't she look beautiful? It's a sad smile, but it's a genuine one. This is the face of a woman ready to risk her life. That's how important it was for her to have you, Ryoko."

Ohhhh. She had forgotten, but now the recognition wandered into her mind. It melted into the real world, connecting: That sad smile Ayame had given her when she and Takemi wandered into that sinister night. The smile her mother had in that old picture, risking her life. Ryoko understood it now. She knew why that smile had stuck in her mind.

Takemi had seen it, as well. Now, she knew why he hadn't paid it any attention.

Ryoko understood everything. She had been the only one capable of understanding that expression.

Oh, Ryoko thought, blearily. *That's it. I get it now, Ayame . . .*

And that's when Ayame stepped in front of Utsume.

It all happened so quickly.

Kijou pointed the gun at Utsume—but just before Kijou squeezed the trigger, Takemi saw Ayame step in front of the Dark Prince, spreading out her arms and shielding him.

"Wha—" Takemi gasped.

Utsume's eyes opened wide, as well, as if even he had not been expecting Ayame's action.

The trigger had been pulled already; there was a gunshot.

Red spray from Ayame's head splashed onto Utsume's chest.

Ayame's body shook before toppling over in slow motion.

Takemi saw it.

The instant Ayame stepped in front of him and Kijou pulled the trigger, the agent's expression turned to one of abject fear.

"Oh n—" his scream vanished.

Ayame's figure popped and was gone. The unnatural spectacle that occurred where she had been swallowed Kijou's scream: The world exploded.

Moments after the bullet hit Ayame's head, Ayame and the space around her popped like a balloon. That really was the best description. It was as though Ayame and the landscape around her had been painted on the side of a giant balloon, and Kijou had just stuck a needle in it.

The world burst open.

The air peeled back, revealing the true landscape underneath.

In a second, the world changed color.

In that moment, our world became the other.

His ears were ringing terribly. Takemi was standing on the school grounds, in the park, beneath the blooming cherry trees.

The blossoms were white. White flowers above, white petals covering the ground, black trunks in rows.

There was a blue bench placed nearby.

Everyone was standing around him, at school, in the park.

Takemi looked up at the night sky.

The sky was very red. In the red sky, the moon glistened like a giant eyeball.

The light from this grotesque moon cast long shadows from the trees, from all of them.

Their shadows were red.

Red shadows stretched from the base of the trees, from their feet, across the ground.

Long and red. The grass beneath them had lost its green tinge. The grass and leaves were washed out, still living, but colored as if they had withered and died.

Red darkness, the color of lost life—it was like a parody of their world done in bad taste.

His ears rang.

The air pressure must be different. The air itself was different, Takemi could tell. Everyone could.

The air smelled different. It was very dry, with a powerful odor of withered grass mixed with a hint of iron. Takemi hadn't breathed anything like it in his life. No, perhaps, he had—that night, when he first encountered *them,* had he caught a whiff of it?

When the world had burst and the colors changed, this air had drifted in from somewhere, surrounding them in an instant. It was the air of an insane world.

His ears adjusted and stopped ringing. And the first sound he heard was a scream.

Kijou was screaming.

Kijou was staring at one spot, his face twisted with fear, screaming.

Kijou was staring at the spot where Ayame had been.

Ayame was no longer there. She had burst and vanished with the space around her.

But Kijou kept his eyes fixed on that spot, as if he could see something, shrieking.

Kijou's face was red.

In the spot where Ayame had been—where there was nothing but empty space now—a red shadow remained, as if Ayame were still standing there.

The shadow covered Kijou as he screamed in terror.

The wind blew.

A gust of wind swept down from the moon, sending cherry

blossoms flying, petals swirling around them in the air, healing that twisted landscape. When the gust had passed, the world was back to normal.

The moon, the sky, the shadows, the grass—everything was back to the original color. And, as if the wind had carried it away, the other world's air was gone, as well.

Takemi closed his eyes, protecting them from the flowers and sand the wind carried. They all closed their eyes, crouching down, waiting for the wind to pass.

Takemi could feel sinister things wriggling around him.

His ears rang again.

Takemi opened his eyes. The world was back to normal. The school was normal again. Not everything was back to normal, though: Ayame was still missing. And there was no sign of Kijou, either.

When the wind swept away the other world, it took Kijou with it.

Cherry blossoms drifted as if nothing had happened.

The night was quiet again.

He heard a sob.

Aki was sitting on the ground, her shoulders shaking.

"I'm the . . . stupid one," she murmured, crying.

Takemi was oddly surprised. He'd never seen her cry before.

"I didn't know anything. I didn't think things through at all. I'm such an idiot! I didn't mean for any of this to happen. I'd have been better off doing nothing at all," she sobbed.

Takemi had no answer for Aki's tragic whisper. Too many things had happened at once, and his mind was worn out.

He turned his head and found Utsume, slumped on the

ground, his head down.

Takemi couldn't make out Utsume's face, but the Dark Prince's hands were pressed flat on the ground.

The ground was white in the moonlight, and Utsume's hands were touching a smattering of dark red specks . . . Ayame's blood.

His hands pressed into it, his shoulders shaking.

"Your Majesty . . . ?" Takemi stammered. He felt like he was watching something he shouldn't have been witness to.

Utsume's shaking was getting stronger. Soon, they could hear his voice: "Heh . . . heh heh . . . heh heh . . . hee hee hee hee hee hee . . . !"

He was laughing. Utsume's shoulders were shaking from laughter.

Takemi gaped at him.

Utsume's shoulders shook a while longer, and then the shaking subsided, and Utsume stood up abruptly.

His normal, impassive poker face had returned.

"Your Majesty . . ." Takemi said gingerly. Utsume turned toward him, looking just as he always had.

"What are you doing, Kondou? Call an ambulance."

His voice did not contain a trace of anything that had just happened.

"Huh?" Takemi said stupidly, unable to comprehend this non sequitur.

"Murakami's leg is broken. He can't exactly walk home, can he? And the girls aren't in good condition. It's up to you to call the ambulance."

When Takemi still failed to react, Utsume glared at him. "What?"

"Um . . . uh . . ."

"You have a cell phone, right?"

"Um, yeah, I do."

"Then hurry," Utsume said, permitting no argument.

Takemi pulled out his phone and dialed the emergency number quickly. He guessed he would be spending quite some time explaining the situation.

Utsume did nothing else. He just sat back down on the bench. He inhaled deeply through his nose, looking oddly regretful.

Chapter Seven

After the Banquet

One

Ayame had been a stepchild, and the world always had seemed out of reach for her. She had fled from rejection into her imagination, eventually being captured by a kami-kakushi. Even that didn't seem to change her distance from the world; although the world she lived in had changed, she still was unwanted.

She had been given eternal isolation. And though she was used to isolation, it still hurt to lose someone once a friendship had been made. She met other people like her, but contact with her always led to their being consumed by the other world.

Her nature was to take those who had the other world in their hearts to that other place. Ayame had been given that power. No. Ayame had *become* that power.

Ayame had become the thing that had taken her.

Ayame abandoned all contact with humans. She could bear her fate, but she could not bear the grief and despair experienced by the people left behind.

That grief and despair served a purpose: It left behind legends, which were passed on in frightened whispers. This was the purpose of Ayame's existence, to create such legends. Ayame's body was no longer human; if she were forgotten, she would vanish forever.

She hadn't minded. Until she met *him*.

Feeling her power weaken, Ayame dreamed of reality.

"My sixth sense is nothing like you imagined. All I can do is smell things that are not from this world, nothing else," Utsume explained to everyone gathered in the club room.

It was one week later.

The ambulance Takemi had called had taken all five of them to the hospital; only Toshiya was injured seriously enough to be hospitalized, though.

The doctors seemed puzzled as to what they all had been doing on the school grounds at night, but none of them offered explanation—for the simple reason that none of them could think of a decent way to explain.

All of them had steeled themselves for a lecture from the police, but none of them could think of a good story.

Ryoko was more frightened of being expelled by the school than being lectured by the police.

They'd all spent an anxious night. Then, two days had passed, and neither the police nor the school said a word.

They all were puzzled but decided not to risk asking about it.

A few days later, Murakami was released from the hospital with a cast. He said, "My parents came to see me . . . apparently, we were helping the police find Utsume."

That explained things.

That's the story the world had been given, so nobody said anything, and the school let them come back without a problem. Someone had taken care of things to prevent stories of the other world from circulating.

Although it was kind of sinister, it played out the way they wanted it to, so they went along with it. Even if they had shouted the truth from the rooftops, nobody would have listened.

And now, it was a week later.

After school, they all gathered together for the first time since that night, crowding around Utsume in the cafeteria, talking.

All of them had different information, and none of them had known exactly what was going on.

Only Utsume seemed to lack interest in the topic. At everyone's insistence, however, he'd agreed to tell his side of things. Reluctantly.

"My sixth sense is not especially strong. I almost never *see* anything. The only unusual thing about me is my sense of smell. No matter how faint, I always can sniff out things that aren't from this world. I assume this is because of my experience as a child. I started smelling that kind of thing shortly after the incident," Utsume explained.

"When I was a child, I met a kami-kakushi. While I was with the kami-kakushi, I was blindfolded and could see nothing. The only thing I can remember is the feeling of something holding my hand. I was blindfolded, and my hearing was not working normally. In that state, I walked through the other world.

"I knew almost nothing about that world. The thing I remembered is the way things smelled. My aromatic memory is the only part of me that accurately recalls the other world.

"So, it isn't really a sixth sense at all. I just recognize the smell of the other world. It's not worth calling it a sixth sense. It doesn't really work that well."

Utsume rarely put himself down like this. He was speaking in level tones, though, as if simply stating the facts.

There was a short silence.

"That's how you found her?" Aki asked, not so much questioning as confirming.

"Exactly," Utsume nodded. "Her clothes and hair were steeped in the scent of that world. Otherwise, I wouldn't have noticed her."

"I see," Aki nodded.

Aki had not come to school for two days. She'd been half-crazed when they'd reached the hospital—and had been hospitalized for a day, completely out of it. Then, she had spent two days locked in her apartment.

Aki was very proud. A display as embarrassing as that made everyone wonder if they would see her again.

Their suspicions were closer to reality than they realized.

But on the third day, Aki slunk guiltily back to school. "Sorry," she said once. Everyone thought she was very strong.

"I was taken by the kami-kakushi," Utsume continued, "and led around the other world for a very long time. I couldn't see anything through the blindfold, but I knew instantly I was no longer in this world. The air smelled wrong. Midsummer never smells of withered grass," Utsume continued.

"Withered?" Takemi said, suddenly leaning forward. "Is that . . . ?"

"You noticed? The smell of the other world that Ayame gave off. That is the world Ayame lives in. It was my first time seeing it, but Ayame smelled faintly of the air from that world. It brought back old memories, so I wanted her."

"'Wanted,' Your Majesty . . . ?"

"That's why I took Ayame around to meet everyone. I thought it might be possible to bring a kami-kakushi over to this side."

"That's why she was your 'girlfriend,' Dark Prince? I knew something was up," Ryoko said with the sort of smile that left no doubt what was on her mind. Afterward, Takemi discovered that Ryoko called her lurid fantasies "romance."

"Part of the experiment," Utsume declared. "I had a younger brother, and he was taken by the kami-kakushi, as well. My brother was spirited away, taken somewhere where there were a lot of other people. He never came home. . . . Ever since, I've wondered if that was the key. My logic was as follows: The more people that are aware of you, the more solid your existence becomes. And this seemed to be a good chance to test that theory. If I introduced her as my girlfriend, it would make a very strong impression, right? That was my goal. Nothing else."

"Well, it was surprising," Ryoko said, looking disappointed. She really had been looking forward to Utsume's romance.

"It did make an impact. Especially with her name being the same as mine," Takemi said carelessly.

Utsume suddenly grimaced. "Oh, that was a big mistake."

"Huh?" Takemi gaped.

Utsume frowned. "A mistake."

"What was?"

"The name," Utsume said, irritated. "She doesn't really have a name. She's not human. I was furious with myself for being such an idiot. It didn't occur to me until you asked. Obviously, when you first meet people in Japan, you call them by their family name."

"And you hadn't picked one?"

"Not only that, but my mind went blank and I couldn't think of any last names. Occasionally, I begin to wonder if I have any common sense at all."

"Well, that does sound like you," Takemi laughed.

Aki laughed, too. "True enough."

As Aki said, despite his immense knowledge, Utsume occasionally would turn out not to know something amazingly simple, and they all found it difficult to believe.

"To cover, I was forced to use Kondou's name. He was right in front of me, and I thought it might make a bigger impact. The

stronger impression she made, the easier it would be to draw her into this world."

"It worked."

"You always have been a good improviser," Aki said, somewhere between impressed and exasperated.

"If your theory was wrong, though, what had you planned to do?" Toshiya said, glaring down at his cast. "Wasn't it dangerous?"

Toshiya had sustained the only serious bodily injury, and it would be several months before he recovered.

There was one other victim, but there was no proof of it. Kijou's disappearance had not been questioned; and when they checked, a different priest was working at Shuzenji.

The new priest was an elderly man, a temporary appointment on loan to the temple after the previous priest had asked to move. He'd had no idea where Kijou might be.

Whether he knew it or not, Utsume had been very close to ending up the same way. This was what Toshiya had meant by his comment about the danger.

"No," Utsume said, emotionless. "Every experiment has its risks. Being alive is a risk in itself. You live while you're alive; and when it's time to die, you die. All of us will die one day, without exception. Where is the problem?"

"Ah, forget it," Toshiya said, giving up. He waved a hand. "I know well enough I can't win this argument."

He didn't want to make a big deal out of it, apparently.

"True," Aki laughed. "So then, what about it?" she asked meaningfully. "Was your theory correct?"

"Oh, about that . . ." Utsume said, turning around, "I have proven that it was correct. The proof is right in front of you."

"Yes," Ayame said. Tears welled up, blurring her vision.

Ayame stood behind him, tears streaming down her face.

A breeze flitted by, carrying with it the scent of spring . . . and faintly, very faintly, the smell of withered grass.

Afterword

First, I'd like to thank you for picking up this book.

Then, I'd like to thank anyone who had anything to do with the book—especially my editors, Mine and Wada, and the illustrator [of the version in print in Japan], Midorikawa. At the moment, I'm still living off my job at an *Imagawa-yaki* restaurant, but these people make it all worthwhile.

So . . .

Have you ever thought about what the world actually is?

What is the world, what are people, what is life, what is death, what is the heart, what is awareness, what are good and evil? Have you ever spent time toying with such unanswerable questions about the concepts our world is built upon?

I have. I think about that kind of thing all the time. Before I know it, I've tuned out the real world.

I'm an idiot.

Because I'm an idiot, I tune out literature.

I'm an incredible idiot.

So, my story is for all the boys and girls who have tuned out the real world—and literature—and for everyone, including myself, who was once that way.

Ah ha ha! Blithering in this way makes me sound cool. But is there anything more embarrassing than an idiot boasting about his stupidity?

If the book sells well, it's because the cover looks pretty. Have you forgotten that the writing only became worth anything because the editors took time out of their busy schedule to prod the stubborn, ignorant writer into making things work? Did you forget that you worked all day long at your day job, phoning the editor up at eleven in the evening? You're the worst kind of newbie. And I've no excuse for spouting off like this.

Soon, everyone will have forgotten me, and I'll die cold and alone. But I don't want to be forgotten, and I've never had much interest in dying cold and alone, so I hope my life doesn't end here. . . .

— Gakuto Coda, April 2001

Coming Soon . . .

Letter of Misfortune

The second book of this intriguing,
thirteen-volume series will arrive
in stores in March 2008!

That day, Aki arrived at school at the beginning of fifth period.

When he saw her coming into the lunch room with a sports bag on her shoulder, Takemi called out, "Ah, Kidono! Over here!"

"Hi," she said, her voice so deep it seemed to rumble upward from hell. She clearly was in a foul mood.

All the Literature Club juniors were gathered in the cafeteria, eating lunch.

Long tables, painted white, stood in rows. During the mid-day break, the clean yet drab cafeteria was crammed with students. And more than one student quickly grew frustrated with jamming themselves into this crowd.

A number of them began seeking alternatives—spending the money and time to head into town to eat or bringing their own lunches. Once they became juniors, students' schedules were more flexible, and people began to shift their lunchtime.

Seisou was a prep school run on the credit system, so weekday classes ran seven periods. An incredible number of classes were offered.

Freshmen were locked into a number of required classes, but after that it was easy enough for students to leave fourth or fifth period open, freeing up time to eat while the cafeteria was almost empty.

The Literature Club juniors all had coordinated their schedules, leaving the fifth period as open as possible. This way, they could meet up during break or fifth period and eat together—as they had done today.

"Aki, I heard you were hurt?" Ryoko called out worriedly as Aki approached.

"Nah, I'm fine," she said, putting down her heavy, textbook-laden bag.

Ryoko had told them all earlier that Aki had hurt herself the night before and had gone to the hospital first thing in the morning.

It wasn't anything serious, apparently, but her injury had started to hurt in the morning, so Aki figured she was better off safe than sorry. She had phoned Ryoko that morning to explain why she would be late.

The bandage around her left hand was proof of her injury.

"How did you hurt yourself?"

"Paper cut."

"Paper?"

"Yep. It was a deeper cut than it first appeared to be. Started to hurt when I woke up—'festering,' they said."

"Huh," Takemi interjected, oddly impressed. He'd never heard of a paper cut becoming so serious before. "Is it okay?"

"I already said it was. It's not my writing hand, anyway."

"Good! We already have Murakami hurt. If you were, too, it might start a trend."

"Thanks," Toshiya replied sarcastically, scowling.

These things always came in threes. Toshiya Murakami had broken his leg in April. It was no longer in a cast, but he was still on crutches. Having too much energy, Toshiya had gone to town with them, and they'd had to reset the break at least once.

"Forget my injury," Aki said grumpily. It appeared something else was the source of her bad mood. "You know Yanagawa, from classical lit? He really pisses me off."

"Oh." That would explain everything. Yanagawa was a widely despised teacher.

Aki made a snarling noise.

She'd missed morning classes and so had visited each of her teachers to explain why and to get copies of any handouts. The teacher for her fourth period class, Yanagawa, had been remarkably spiteful.

A gaunt man who always wore silver-rimmed glasses, Yanagawa was an ordinary teacher to students who blended in. But once a student caught his attention, he became astonishingly mean, and he never let up. Most of his students hated him. And the fact that it was impossible to get out of taking his classical literature course just made things worse.

Takemi didn't care for him, either. He'd fallen asleep in Yanagawa's class once. "'Of course, you understand something this basic, don't you, sleepy Kondou?' It's Yanagawa's favorite phrase. Augh. I'm getting worked up by the memory alone. I'm sure he still remembers it!"

"He keeps that up all day."

"He still says something when I run into him in the hall!"

"Augh."

Ryoko and Takemi sighed in unison. Neither had enjoyed his classes.

"And now you, too?" Ryoko said sympathetically.

"But His Majesty and Murakami never had any problems with him, right?" Takemi asked.

Both refuted that statement quickly.

"Not true," Utsume said. "He thought I had a bad attitude, hated me for ignoring him."

"He got me while I was on crutches."

"Too many ways to count."

"Yep."

It seemed as if he had it in for all five of them.

"Well, at least we're all equal?" Ryoko murmured.

Utsume snorted. He was skeptical of concepts such as equality or impartiality. Ryoko could remember him saying that he didn't believe equality was either realistic or just.

"S-so that's just the way he is. May as well ignore him!" Ryoko said with fruitless cheer. "The only one of us he isn't after is Ayame!"

"Well, yeah," Takemi said. Ayame never went to class, and she wasn't even a student, so how was a teacher supposed to know about her or go after her?

When her name was mentioned, Ayame jumped nervously.

Aki pressed her fingers to her temples. "Right," she said, as if acknowledging her doomed state. "Even if Yanagawa had been an asshole to every single person alive, that has nothing to do with me. He could insult every living thing if he wants to, but it wouldn't clear him of the sins he committed against me today. Does any of this talk change the fact that even your classmates call you 'sleepy' now?"

"Eh? Um . . ."

"No, not really."

"Then, don't pretend it does," Aki snapped. "Besides, I hardly would be this pissed off just because a cretin like Yanagawa had been a little rude."

Takemi didn't believe that for a second, but he decided to keep that retort to himself because he had no idea how Aki might respond to it. Instead, he asked, "Was there something else?"

"Yeah," Aki said, opening her bag.

She slapped a pile of paper down on the table. It was curled up, so Takemi reached out to press it flat.

"Fax paper?"

"Yep," she said. It was, indeed, laser-printer paper: thin paper with a little gloss on the surface, letter size, and about ten pages long by appearance. It was nothing out of the ordinary, merely typical fax paper. However . . .

"What is this?"

One look at it was enough to identify it as odd.

Every page was covered in a sinister scrawl. Letters of the alphabet were scribbled tightly together, one after the other, vowels and constants not forming anything like words.

It went on and on—and on. It was as if the pages were covered in insects. The very sight made Takemi's skin crawl.

AAhaaAaurruaaaaaaaaAAAaAAAAAAAAer/TteeieeeeeerehiierrrEE Eeereeeeieeeeeeeeeereee//MMaaaAhhhhaaaaAAaauuaaaaaaaaaaR RruuUUUuouuuuuuvvvvvvvvvvu/KKKhuuuouRuuuuouRuuuiurra aavruuuuuuUUUt//Vee/geeaHaaEEeEeeeeeruuaeEEEEjjeeeeeeeeeE yy/BvuuuurRRRUuuvvvvvbbuuVuuuuuaaahaaaAaaaAaaaaaaaa aaaaahh//Vee/Geeeeeeeeeeeeeeeeeeeeeeeeeehe/BdryuuUuuRLuuhaa AAAAaaaharearRRrrruaaaAAAAAAAHHAAAAAEa/RUyUU/uO OOOOOOOOouuruuuuuuuaaaaayaaahhhhaAAAAArrrRMMM MMUUUUouuuuuuuuuaMuu/eAaaaaaaaaaaaaaaaaahMeeeeeeeee eeeeeeeeeeeeMmnnnnnnnnnnnnnnnnnNn . . .

The sheer weirdness of it silenced them all.

The air-conditioning was not the only reason they felt cold.

Even Murakami was frowning. Utsume calmly picked up the pages and looked over them, but this probably was because he was fundamentally different from everyone else, psychologically speaking.

"What is it?" Ryoko said, obviously creeped out.

"It was faxed to me last night," Aki said.

Her machine had whirred to life suddenly in the middle of the night, at two o'clock in the morning.

Aki lived alone, in an apartment, making getting something like this particularly nasty.

Students who weren't born locally were not at all unusual here; but the school had perfectly nice dormitories, so most students lived there. To live alone like Aki did was extremely rare, but she had her reasons.

Whatever those reasons were, this still was a malicious sort of prank. After all, Aki was a girl, living alone. Takemi wasn't either one—even so, he was sure he'd be in for a bout of sleeplessness if he received something like this in the middle of the night.

There were thirteen pages covered in hundreds or perhaps thousands of letters. The rows of roughly written, tightly packed letters were daunting enough; but more frightening was the existence of the kind of mind it took to do something like this, the sheer passion it must've taken to fill thirteen pages of letter-sized paper this way. The rows of letters broke off here and there; each time, there was a big cross scribbled onto the page. Above each big cross was another, smaller cross.

It was terrifying.

Imagining a madman writing furiously in a dark room, Takemi allowed himself a shiver of revulsion.

"The sender's number is 'unknown,'" Murakami remarked, lighting onto something practical. "Some kind of stalker?"

"How would I know?" Aki said, disgusted. "I brought it along— but mostly, I just wanted to gripe. Truth be told, I almost threw out the whole thing, but then I thought it might be evidence."

She already was prepared to take this to the police.

"Probably a good idea," Toshiya said. "And you also can call the phone company to stop receiving faxes from unidentified numbers."

"Mm? Oh, yeah. But . . ." Aki said, suddenly reluctant to speak.

For no real reason, this bothered Takemi.

There was a long silence. The bustle of the fifth-period cafeteria carried on around them.

"Oh, wait!" Ryoko said.

"Mm? What?"

"I've heard about this. It's kind of like the Letter of Misfortune."

"Oh," Takemi said, remembering. He'd heard of it, too.

Everyone else looked blank. Only Takemi and Ryoko had heard the story.

"The cursed fax," Takemi whispered.

The cursed fax.

He couldn't remember who had told him about it.

The basic idea was similar to the Letter of Misfortune: One day, a mysterious fax would come to your house, and if you didn't send it to someone else . . . It was kind of cliché.

The story had spread among teenagers here in Hazama, and someone had sent a postcard to a radio show about it.

The bulk of the fad had happened about six months prior. Nobody had died in Hazama yet, but there were stories about someone who'd died in Tokyo after failing to send it on.

It was a stupid story, yet oddly believable. It sounded as if some people actually had received the fax, too.

The exact details were as follows:

The cursed fax comes at two in the morning.
If you receive the first one, it will come for seven nights.
If you receive the final fax . . .
Then, starting the next day, at the same time . . .
You must fax it to someone else, in the same order.
If you do not, or you get the order wrong . . .
The curse will take effect and you will die.

"Ridiculous."

Aki's opinion was exactly what Takemi had expected.

"Anyone who believes crap like that ought to have his head examined. It's absurd! We're not children, for God's sake. We have better things to do!" she spat. Her eyes were hard like steel.

"You don't need to tell me," Takemi quailed.

Takemi was seated directly opposite Aki, and her fury was so palpable that he grew frightened, despite knowing she wasn't directing her rage at him specifically.

He was somewhat ashamed of his own weakness, but it was bad for his heart to see people really, genuinely angry. He would prefer to avoid contact with them. Yet here he was.

"I mean, they might not actually believe it," he said, trying to appease her.

"Then, it's just a prank? That's worse!"

Clearly, he'd dug himself deeper. Takemi decided to stop talking.

He glanced at the others for help, but they were staring at the fax pages, thinking. None of them made eye contact.

215

"Heartless . . ." Takemi grimaced.

"Do these letters mean anything?" Ryoko asked.

Apparently, she had overcome her initial fear and was staring at a few of the pages.

"I can't read it at all. It doesn't look like English. Is it French?"

"Of course not," Aki snapped.

Despite this, Ryoko looked pleased with herself. For a second, Takemi was extremely jealous of her.

"Ah ha ha! I was kidding. These are impossible to pronounce, though. How do you even read them? Aahaaauruaaaaaaaaaaa—"

"Stop it. You're embarrassing yourself."

"The crosses are creepy, too—like they want you to die."

"Don't say things like that."

"Sorry. But what else could they mean? That's what the cross *is*."

Aki pulled her face into a sour expression, but she had to admit that Ryoko was right.

Takemi looked at Ryoko, and she winked at him.

Oh, he thought. She'd changed the subject to free him from Aki's rage. He raised a hand, quietly thanking her. He felt sorry for Aki but was glad to have his friends there.

Ryoko grinned back. Then, she turned to the others. "Am I right or what?"

"Yeah," Takemi nodded, agreeing.

She may have been trying to change the subject, but she still had a point. It was the only meaning Takemi could come up with, too.

Just as everyone seemed to agree . . .

"No, that would be incorrect." Utsume broke his silence, dismissing her theory.

"Eh?"

"There is a tendency to connect the cross to gravestones and view it as a symbol of death, but that actually is not true—that usage is secondary to the original meaning," he said flatly.

Everyone looked interested.

"There's a field of anthropology called 'symbolic anthropology,'" Utsume said, closing his eyes as he always did when remembering something. "All patterns occurring in the world contain hidden cultural meaning. Have you all forgotten? The cross is a Christian symbol. It normally serves as a symbol of the son of God, who was crucified upon it. As a symbol of that religion, it has come to symbolize faith and the church—but it originally meant 'atonement,' which of course, goes hand in hand with 'salvation.' That's why it's also used to symbolize hospitals. Stretching it still further, it symbolizes anything 'holy.' That's what it means in magic. Late-period magic is a product of Christian culture, so a lot of magicians use the cross in that sense. Additionally, just from the shape alone, it can be used to symbolize a person."

"Huh."

"Of course, it also means 'death.' But burial beneath a gravestone means 'death under faith'—in other words, ascension to heaven. It wasn't originally a negative meaning at all; but since death itself is repellent, I wouldn't call it a positive meaning, either. This is Japan, though, and Christian thought is not exactly the basis of our society, so it's only natural to take it to mean 'death.' Except . . ."

And here, Utsume took a breath.

". . . in this case, it's more likely 'Purification with a Qabalistic Cross.'"

They hadn't ever heard the terms he concluded with.

Not understanding, Takemi echoed, "Kaba . . . listic? What?"

"'Purification with a Qabalistic Cross.' It's a magical ritual," Utsume explained, not showing any particular interest.

"Magic?"

"Yes. It's a type of magical ritual, a cleansing ritual performed before and after other rituals. Magicians use it to remove spiritual impurities and fill themselves with spiritual power. Considering that it's performed before and after any magical ritual, it can be found in many books aimed at the neophyte magician. It's the most basic magic ritual, and it must be learned by anyone beginning to experiment with magic."

"This is . . . ?" Takemi said, frowning at the fax. He couldn't connect Utsume's perfunctory explanation with the terrifying thing in front of them.

"Yes," Utsume nodded. "The words on this fax are all broken apart—then, there's the spacing of the letters, rows, even the use of upper and lower case letters. At first glance, it appears to be completely random. But look here: The groups of letters between the crosses all begin with A and end with N. The pattern of letters within each is identical. You can't pronounce it spelled like this, but . . . chances are, these are the Hebrew holy words chanted during the ritual."

"H-hebrew?"

"Ateh malkuth ve-geburah ve-gedulah le-olam, amen," Utsume said. "When chanting, people often stretch out the vowels and the final sounds, so it would end up being pronounced just like it's written here. It means: Thou art the kingdom and the power and the glory forever. When performing the ritual, a magician chants this while tracing a cross in the air, holding a real dagger or his fingers in the sign of the sword, like this—" He held up his hand, with only the index and middle fingers extended: the sign of the sword.

"They trace a cross with each recitation of the holy words. That suggests the big crosses mean tracing the cross, whereas the smaller crosses above them are the sword itself. During the purification, the sword begins in the same location, above the head. The magician begins by imagining the sun above his head and next, touching it with the sword."

As he spoke, Utsume raised his hand above his head. He still was holding it in the sign of the sword.

"They say the magic words: Ateh . . ." His fingers touched his forehead.

"Malkuth . . ." His chest.

"Ve-geburah . . ." His right shoulder.

"Ve-gedulah . . ." His left shoulder.

"Le-olam, amen." He finished with both hands clasped before his chest.

"It's a very simple ritual, so that concludes it. If the magician combines this with proper breathing and visualization, it will cleanse him spiritually. This is just conjecture on my part, but I image 'spiritual impurity' has much the same meaning, in practice, as idle thoughts."

"Huh."

"Magic in actual practice is very different from the popular image of it. Modern magicians neither fly nor throw fire. The main goal of magic actually is to alter the magician's own consciousness. The most famous magicians of the modern age—people like Mathers, Crowley, Fortune—all of them considered this discipline to be the basis of magic. These magicians believed their wills could influence reality; but unless they could control their own minds, it was meaningless. The rituals all were designed with this in mind. Even the 'demons' were simply a symbol used for that purpose."

So, magic meant the use of ritual to transform the practitioner's consciousness. And the elevation of the mind was the same thing as the practice of magic, Utsume explained.

Takemi was surprised to hear this, considering he'd always connected magic with bloody sacrifices, horrible demons, and sinister, bubbling cauldrons.

But the magic Utsume described seemed much more refined—more like an ascetic monk, and nothing dangerous about it at all.

"So this fax isn't bad?" Takemi asked.

Utsume shook his head. "I never said it was good or bad, only that magic was a technique for altering one's own consciousness."

It seemed the question confused him.

"Eh? But if magic means elevating yourself, then it has nothing to do with, say, curses."

"Clearly, your thoughts are unable to get past the term 'magic.'" Utsume sighed. His gaze wavered, searching for words. "Then, let's switch the terminology to *budo*. The way of the warrior also is designed to better yourself—but if used with the intention to hurt people, those same techniques become extremely dangerous, right?"

"Right . . ."

"Magic is the same. If your intentions and will are evil, and you perform magic—then, naturally it can be incredibly dangerous."

"Mm . . ."

"You see? Magic can be both beneficial and destructive. To use an awful phrase, there is both 'white' and 'black' magic.

Both are magic, and both use the same techniques, but those are merely tools to be used at the magician's discretion. Magic itself has no inherent moral bias. If you immediately assume sinister intentions when you hear the term 'magic,' you stand to make a terrible mistake."

"Wow. Okay."

"You linked the word 'magic' to evil. When I dismissed that, you instantly leapt to good. This merely proves that you are overly influenced by the image of magic planted in your mind by Christianity: an extreme dualism. The first thing we must do here is stop attempting to decide if things are good or evil. Those concepts are poorly defined to begin with."

"All right."

He had leapt to conclusions, clearly. Magic depended on who was using it, clearly.

Takemi picked up the fax.

"So which is this?" That was all he wanted to know. Was this fax dangerous? Not dangerous? That was the the whole point.

When Takemi asked, Utsume looked pleased, as if he'd finally heard the right question. "Dangerous."

"Thought so."

"The purification ritual itself is merely a preparation, something done before beginning the actual spell. The problem lies in the caster's intentions. The exact same ritual performed with different intentions will have the opposite effect. From the sinister nature of this writing style alone, it obviously is intended to cause harm," Utsume said firmly.

Ryoko spoke up, suddenly worried. "Is Aki really okay? Did anything strange happen?"

"Nothing."

"Really . . . ?"

"Yeah," Aki snapped, annoyed.

Ryoko wasn't ready to let it drop. "Is she gonna be okay, Dark Prince?"

Utsume shrugged. "We presently have no idea what the sender was trying to do, so I can't say. I *can* say that the contents of the fax resemble a magical ritual, but I don't deny that this might be a coincidence. Even if it is the Purification of the Qabalistic Cross, we have no way of knowing if the sender is a magician or just a stalker who happens to have read a book or two on magic. If it's a stalker, we also can't tell if it will remain just a prank or escalate into something more dangerous."

"But that's—"

"And it might've been faxed to the wrong number. The degree of danger is currently completely unknown. Still . . ." Utsume said, glancing at the fax again.

"The sender of this fax does seem to wish harm to the recipient—or at least harbors some kind of twisted feelings for her. Even if it has nothing to do with magic, that much is obvious," he said, dismissing his own exposition.

Without magic, it was just as it appeared to be, like they all had known from the very beginning.

"Your Highness . . ."

"That's more than enough, isn't it? Make sure to lock your doors and windows," Utsume said practically.

"But . . ."

"What? If it is magic, it's pointless to do anything."

"Why?"

"Why?" Utsume echoed, frowning. "I never once said magic actually was effective."

"Huh?" Takemi gaped at him.

"I possess a certain degree of knowledge about magic, but I've never tried to use it, and I don't believe that it actually works. Any attempts to counter it would be absurd."

Takemi had nothing else to say. Feeling as if every assumption he'd been making had been overturned, he became almost dizzy.

Of course, once he thought about it, Utsume was right. Utsume had been giving only his analysis of the fax's contents, which had nothing to do with whether curses and magic were actually real. The idea that Aki was being cursed was entirely a product of Takemi's mind.

At some point, he'd gotten carried away in the sheer atmosphere of Utsume's lecture.

"Out of all of us, you'd be the easiest to curse, Kondou," Utsume announced.

"W-why?"

"Curses have a lot in common with hypnotism. In primitive societies, when a well-known wizard put a curse on someone, he'd always go and tell the person. Then, he'd put on a performance to suggest the casting of the curse. But that was not a ritual, not a prayer, nothing of the kind. It was simply this: With that knowledge, the cursed man becomes nervous. After all, a man everyone knows is a powerful wizard has just cursed him, and this fact is a powerful suggestion. The cursed believes the spell will kill him. Then, it's a placebo effect. Even without the existence of an actual curse, through the sheer power of suggestion, the cursed man often would die."

"Urr."

"See, Kondou? That's how curses work. I don't mind that you're simple-minded—but if you believe anything people tell you, without any skepticism, you'll end up being killed by something that *doesn't even exist.*"

It sounded like a threat.

Takemi gulped.

Aki burst out laughing. "Ah ha ha. Simple-minded? You got that right."

"What?" Takemi said.

"Ha ha! Sorry." Aki stood up. "Sorry. I'm just a little wound up. I know the fax is just a prank. Forget about it. It's nothing."

She flipped her bag onto her shoulders. The others looked at the clock and realized fifth period was almost over.

"Kidono," Toshiya said grimly.

"Mm?"

"Be careful."

"I know."

"Especially if it's a stalker. Humans are far more dangerous than any curse. A violent thug will cause much more damage than anything occult. After all, it wasn't Ayame that broke my leg. It was another human." Toshiya tapped his leg, still not fully recovered.

Ayame bowed apologetically.

Aki chuckled. "I agree."

The bell rang, signaling the end of fifth period.

"So . . ."

"Yeah."

And with that, Aki walked away.

With fifteen minutes left until sixth period began, everyone began preparing to leave.

Takemi stood up but noticed that Utsume had a strange expression on his face.

"Something wrong, Your Highness?"

"No," Utsume said. He frowned, and then he took a long, slow breath through his nose. He closed his eyes, thinking, as if something wasn't falling into place. Takemi began to get nervous.

"Can you smell something?"

Utsume didn't answer.

Utsume had a very unusual ability—he could smell things that were not of this world. As a child, he'd been captured by a *kami-kakushi,* and this extraordinary experience left him with this ability. It had led him to Ayame, which in turn led to a very dangerous sequence of events.

According to him, he could not distinguish the smells from real scents at all. They weren't that different from ordinary odors; so, unless the smell was jarringly out of place, he rarely noticed. But occasionally, he would catch a whiff of something that clearly didn't belong. At those times, a being from the other world was nearby.

His ability was absolutely real, and if he smelled something strange, there always was *something there.*

Given what they'd just been talking about, Takemi was right to be worried.

After a long pause, Utsume spoke. "Rot."

"Eh?"

"It's very faint, but I smell rotting meat."

Very unsettling.

"And an animal—some kind of dog, I think. No . . . ?" he crooked his head.

Takemi shuddered. "I-is it . . . *other?*"

"I don't know. Too faint."

"But there's no rotting meat or dogs in the cafeteria."

"Not necessarily," Utsume said. He sniffed again. "No good, it's gone."

Then, he picked up his things and headed off to class.

"Eh? Wait!" Takemi said, hurrying after him.

And for the moment, the matter rested. At that time, they still had no idea what was going on.

To be continued . . .

STOP!

You wouldn't want to spoil a great ending!

The rest of this book is printed "manga-style," in the authentic Japanese right-to-left format. Turn the book over and start again. Since none of the artwork has been flipped or altered, readers get to experience the story just as the creator intended. You've been asking for it, so TOKYOPOP® delivered: authentic, hot-off-the-press, and far more fun!

DIRECTIONS

If this is your first time reading manga-style, here's a quick guide to help you understand how it works.

It's easy... just start in the top right panel and follow the numbers. Have fun, and look for more 100% authentic manga from TOKYOPOP®!

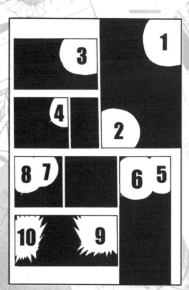

I KNOW!!

SO DON'T START FEELING SORRY FOR SOMEONE WHO'S PROBABLY DEAD ALREADY ANYWAYS!

RIGHT NOW, WE DON'T EVEN KNOW IF YOU'LL EVER SEE YOUR BELOVED PRINCE OF DARKNESS AGAIN!

SHE'S NOT SO BAD, THOUGH.

WE'VE HARDLY EVEN SPOKEN TO HER.

WE DON'T EVEN KNOW HER.

BUT.

BUT...

I KNOW.

THEN THE COURT WILL TREAT HIM TO AN EXECUTION.

IF KYO WENT WITH HER WILLINGLY... BUT ENDS UP NEEDING OUR HELP...

A BRILLIANT PLAN!

BUT...

TO ALL THOSE PEOPLE WHO... DISAPPEAR?

SO, LIKE, WHAT HAPPENS, ANYHOW?

THEY'RE GONE.

カララ

...KNEW WHAT KIND OF DANGER HE WAS IN, AND STILL ACCEPTED THE RISK...

IF KYO...

...HE'S LESS THAN THE GENIUS WE MADE HIM OUT TO BE.

BUT FOR THE MOST PART, THEY'RE JUST GONE. MISSING.

PROBABLY KILLED. SOMETIMES THEIR MUTILATED CORPSES POP UP SOMEWHERE.

LIKE FROM A HORROR MOVIE?!

THAT'S WHAT WE'RE FACING? A SUPER-NATURAL KILLER?

ACCORDING TO KYO'S BOOKS, FEW SOULS, IF ANY, EVER MAKE IT BACK FROM THE OTHER SIDE.

IF IT WERE ANYONE OTHER THAN KYO, I'D HAVE SAID A PRAYER FOR THEM BY NOW, AND GONE ABOUT MY BUSINESS.

HAVE YOU EVER HEARD THE EXPRESSION "SPIRITED AWAY" USED FOR PEOPLE WHO DISAPPEAR WITHOUT A TRACE?

WELL, THEN THEY WOULDN'T CALL THEM KAMIKAKUSHI, WOULD THEY?

IF THEY COULD JUST COME HOME WHEN THEY WANTED TO...

Also Available . . .

Kamikakushi no Monogaatari

Fans of Gakuto Coda's debut novel will appreciate his tale in a wholly different format, accompanied by striking illustrations! Manga-ka Rei Mutsuki is responsible for the beautiful, faithfully rendered graphic novel version of the prose novel you've just finished reading. Turn the page to take a sneak peek at the enticing manga series. . . .

Story by Gakuto Coda
Art by Rei Mutsuki